Adventures
of a
Foot Washer

Adventures
of a
Foot Washer

Carlos Alonso

iUniverse, Inc.
New York Lincoln Shanghai

Adventures of a Foot Washer

iUniverse books may be ordered through booksellers or by contacting:

iUniverse
2021 Pine Lake Road, Suite 100
Lincoln, NE 68512
www.iuniverse.com
1-800-Authors (1-800-288-4677)

ISBN: 978-0-595-47638-1 (pbk)
ISBN: 978-0-595-91902-4 (ebk)

Printed in the United States of America

Contents

Foreword

The speaker's voice rang out with shocking intensity in the convention center: "I am asking, 'How many of you really know God?' I am not asking whether you know about Him? I am asking, 'Do you know Him?'" He paused. It was electrifying. The words burned into my heart. It was as if God had spoken to me personally. It was 1965, and I was one of 5,000 college students attending the Intervarsity Christian Fellowship (IVCF) international missionary conference in Urbana, Illinois.

More than 40 years later I can still hear that ringing question. You see, though president of the IVCF chapter at the University of South Florida, and though I sought to be a good leader for the students who met on campus, my life and ministry were incomplete. I knew it. Power was missing; reality was missing. At the time I could not shout back: "I know Him!" The speaker was right: I knew about the Lord. I knew that my sins were covered by His blood. But He had not yet revealed Himself to me in the power of the Holy Spirit. I knew Jesus was magnificent; but I did not know Him. I tried to fill that void with good works and Christian fellowship; yet I longed, yea, thirsted for the presence of God. For me, praise His name, it was only a few more months until I received the blessed fullness of His Spirit. And what a joy it has been from then until now.

If you are like I was, and hunger for more of God, read *Adventures of a Foot Washer,* for in its pages you will find that Jesus still satisfies the thirsting soul. In the book's simplicity you may come to know the Lord in a deeper way, for *Foot Washer* is a sparkling, wonderful story about a man who, like David, was after God's own heart. It is about Carlos Alonso, and it is magnetically contagious. Many have been encouraged to take up a cross and follow Jesus by the ministry and testimony of Carlos' life. And those who have followed, have found peace and joy.

Like the man, the book is not fancy. More like Elijah than a polished modern evangelist, Carlos views himself as a slave of Jesus, and a foot washing one at that. His passion is to serve the Lord and, in the end, to hear those marvelous words

Well done thou good and faithful servant. Like Paul, Carlos chooses to know *nothing except Jesus Christ and Him crucified.* Yet, his message has, through the years, been certified by *demonstrations of the Spirit and of power, that your faith should not be in the wisdom of men but in the power of God.*

Foot Washer tells of Carlos' call; of the faith the Lord gave him; and of the signs and wonders performed in the Holy Spirit to testify of that call. As you read the pages of this splendid chronicle, you will be able to believe afresh that Jesus fellowships with those who seek Him with their whole heart, and abides in those who hear His call and open the door to Him. Believe, if not for Carlos' story, the works described in it, for they testify of Jesus' anointing for ministry to the poor and needy of this world.

You might ask, "But who is Carlos Alonso?" Many have not heard of him. Carlos was born in Cuba in 1937, the son of Manuel Alonso and Maria C. Suarez. In the pleasant days of childhood, he dreamed of serving God as a teacher of a purer form of religion. But it would be years before God would call him to that work. Until then, there was for Carlos the matter of God's crucible.

Manuel Alonso worked hard on the docks of Havana and wisely invested his significant wages in Cuban real estate. Through his efforts over the years, Manuel prospered. Yet he was among many Cubans who had their wealth ripped away by Castro during the communist revolution. Carlos, then a teenager, left Cuba in bitter rage. Once in the United States, for several years he was actively involved in violent anti-socialist demonstrations, being arrested for fighting more than once.

During this period, he flourished as owner of a thriving beauty salon. Yet, in those turbulent days Carlos began to recognize the need for a deeper relationship with God. So, when the Lord called, he was ready. Carlos responded the only way he knew: with his whole being. He determined to serve the Lord totally, and he felt the best way to do so was to sell his business and walk in faith. Thus, when the Lord said it was time, that is exactly what Carlos did. He sold his business, lived on its proceeds until they ran out, and has lived by faith from then until now. He tells his needs only to the Lord; and for almost 40 years the Lord has sustained him.

Adventures of A Foot Washer is the story of that walk. Woven into the book are lessons the Lord taught Carlos. These instructions are principles upon which his life and faith are based. As his story unfolds, a number of people whom Carlos loves and admires are introduced. These share life with him and hold his hands up to the Lord, even as Aaron and Hur held Moses' hands up as Joshua battled the Amalekites. They laugh and cry with him. To him, they are precious ones in the earth.

Any who long for the reality and presence of God in their own lives will be refreshed by Carlos' story. They will rejoice to see that, still today, the Holy Spirit works as in the book of Acts. They will see God heal, deliver and give life; and they will know that He still pours His Spirit out upon a dry and thirsty land.

Carlos would invite them, as he does all to whom he ministers, "Come, take your fill of Jesus."

Darell B. Dyal
Editor and Friend

Growing in the Faith

This, my second trip to Guatemala, was very special, for the lesson I learned was a compass to follow for the rest of my life.

I arrived late at night in Guatemala City, at the home of pastor Tim Robenstain who was doing mission work there. I had previously met him on my first journey. That night, when I was in bed, the Holy Spirit told me to give all the money I had with me to Tim. At first, I could not figure it out, so I started to rationalize. I thought that it was the enemy talking to me. But, after few minutes I understood that it was the Lord. The money I had was just enough for my expenses there and to buy my plane ticket to return home, because I only had a one-way ticket.

I started to bargain with the Lord, and asked Him if I could keep $150. He said, "No," so I went down to $100, to $75, to $50, to $25, then $10, and finally to $3. Every time He said, "No."

You might wonder why I asked for $3 dollars? It was because I wanted to go to a little town called Chiquimulilla, and the round trip bus ticket was $3.

After my negotiation failed, the Lord asked me, "Whose trip is this?" Then it hit me. I realized that if I kept the money, it would be "my" trip from then on, but if I gave all my money in obedience to Him, it would be "His" trip. In other words, the Lord was teaching me that my dependence had to be completely on Him.

I decided to obey the voice of the Holy Spirit, and as I did, a supernatural peace came over me. I felt the joy of giving with no strings attached. Needless to say, I slept next to heaven that night. The next day someone came to take me to pray for a family seeking the Baptism in the Holy Spirit. It was a family of seven, and all of them received the Baptism with the manifestation of speaking in other tongues. As I was leaving, the father gave me $15 dollars. I thanked him and left. On my way back, I passed an antique shop and noticed two silver crosses that I liked a lot. I asked the owner how much they were, and he said they were not for sale. But at my insistence, he agreed to sell them to me for $13 dollars. As I started to pay, I realized that I really could not buy them, for it would leave me short on the trip to Chiquimulilla. Then I perceived the voice of the Lord telling me to buy, for this was His trip and He was my provider. So I obeyed and bought the crosses.

By the time I got to the house, an envelope was waiting for me from a lady I did not know, whose son I had prayed for in the Hospital. The envelope had exactly $13 dollars inside with a note that said the Lord had laid it on her heart to send the money to me. That night, two individuals came to see me because they wanted to buy any electronic items I might have. All I had was a radio with a tape recorder, but I told them that I was not interested in selling because I wanted to record the messages that I would preach. However, as I was talking to them, the Lord spoke to me and told me to go ahead and sell the radio and tape recorder because He was the one who had sent them to me. He also said not to worry about recording my messages. He explained that, in heaven, good records are kept, and in perfect order, too. So, I sold the recorder for $45.

At that time I was still very young in the faith. I was on the mission field for only the second time, so I earnestly prayed for the gifts of *knowledge* and *wisdom*. Praise His name, by faith I received them! He also gave me a promise from the Scriptures: He said He would go before me and make every crooked way straight.

The next day I went to Chiquimulilla. I was to stay upstairs in the church building. It was very hot and humid, and there were no windows. As I lay down in a hammock to sleep after the long trip, the mosquitoes decided it was time for supper. The pastor (who was to sleep in a hammock in the same room) and I were to be their *main course*. Their attack was vicious! Jesus was our only hope, so we stood against them in His great name. And Jesus delivered us from the raging mosquitoes the same way He delivered Daniel from the lions so long ago. They left us alone! It was a powerful sign to me that I was on the Lord's business and that He was making every way straight.

After it quieted down, the pastor told me what happened to him that day. He said he went to the home of an elderly lady who had been crippled and in bed for over 5 years, and, while he was praying for her she started throwing up. I asked if she was healed, and explained that it was my understanding that when that happens it is because an evil spirit is leaving the body. I told him that she should have been healed after the deliverance and gave him the example of how, on many occasions, Jesus cast out demons and that, after that, there was a healing or miracle. I told him the next day we would go see her together.

The following day, however, the pastor was called to another town, so I ended up going by myself to the old lady's home, which was only three rooms. When I arrived, the Holy Spirit took over, and without my saying a word, the family started to ask forgiveness of one another. Repentant hearts were all over the house (there were about 15 in the family). When I saw this, I knew that the lady would be healed. I proceeded to her bed and laid hands on her and started to rebuke the spirit of infirmity. I spent several minutes calling on the name of Jesus, but to no avail. At that point I stood aside, faced the wall and asked the Lord what was happening? Why was the evil spirit not coming out? I heard the Holy Spirit say, "Nothing is coming out because the demon has already gone." Immediately He reminded me of my prayer in Guatemala City and what He told me. To review, He had promised that He would go before me and straighten my path; and He reminded me about the gifts of the Holy Spirit, *wisdom* and *knowledge*, that I had asked for, and received, by faith.

Then I understood. The pastor had gone ahead of me the day before, and Jesus kept His promise by going there with him in the power of the Holy Spirit. While I was facing the wall, I asked Jesus what I was to do next, and He said, "You prayed for gifts of *wisdom* and *knowledge*. Now use them as needed." On that word, I turned around and went back to her bed. I explained to her what had taken place the day before. Then I led her in a confession of faith that Jesus had already delivered her, and that Satan was the father of lies and that there was no truth in him. She repeated the words after me, and as soon as she finished, I took both of her hands. The power of the Holy Spirit came all over me and passed to her. She got up and walked around and around in the room. Everyone began glorifying the Lord!

After a few minutes, I asked the Holy Spirit what to do next. He told me that He wanted her to be filled with the Holy Spirit, so I laid hands on her and the Holy Ghost power came down and she started to speak in tongues and to dance before the Lord. I was very much taken by the fact that after five years in bed this elderly lady was dancing before the Lord. I wondered about the many people who are perfectly healthy, yet are ashamed to lift their hands in praise to the Lord, much less dance before Him. They may not be physically impaired, but they are crippled spiritually. They say that salvation is a private matter therefore no one ever knows that they are followers of Christ. Yet, salvation is the greatest gift of all!

Needless to say, after this a mighty revival broke out in that town, and many miracles took place. People came from all around to accept Jesus as their personal Savior. Every day we had water baptisms in a nearby river. I remember during the ministry of those days how many times after a service I had to lean against the wall because I was so tired after praying for the crowds of people. It was a labor of love; but it was exhausting nonetheless.

I used to bathe in the same river where the baptisms were held. I remember that, on one occasion, I saw a lady from the church washing her clothes in the river. Though she was bare-breasted, I did not say a word, nor was I offended. You see, the Holy Spirit let me know that I was not there to judge or condemn their customs or culture. I was there to seek and to save those who were lost. For them, that was their natural way of life, and what was sinful to me in my culture was not sinful to them. Besides, it is the Holy Spirit who is responsible to convict of sin, not me, and only when one is convicted of his sins is he accountable for them.

On the day I was to leave Guatemala City, people from the church formed a long single line and the pastor told me that they had come to bless me. They brought money in their hands. At first I did not want to take it, but the Holy Spirit prompted me to do so. Jesus reminded me that, as I had emptied myself of all my money in obedience to Him, so they were obeying Him as well. I started to weep as I looked down at their feet, for many did not even have shoes to wear. After it was over, I counted the money they had given me plus the money from the tape recorder, and it was exactly the amount I needed to buy my return ticket.

Right after I got home, Joanna Heard, who had led me to Jesus, gave me a new tape recorder. The Lord had told her to give it to me. I am sure it was at least three times more valuable than the one I sold in Guatemala City. Even the shoes and clothes I had given were replaced by more than I had before. That trip was on-the-job training for me as I allowed the Holy Spirit to be my teacher all the way. And, as I always say, the Word of God must be put into practice to be effective.

Maybe now, before I tell the rest of the story, it might be the right time to share some of the most important lessons the Lord has taught me, for they are the foundation upon which my life and faith are based. [1] The first is so important He took me through it twice, separated by a number of years. It is this: *In the beginning was the Word, and the Word was with God; and the Word was God. The same was in the beginning with God.* The vital point is that

Jesus is God.

Here is the way it happened. I recall that, right after my conversion, as I was driving home from a Bible study, the Holy Spirit spoke to me very clearly with the same words, "Jesus is God." This happened three times and I repeated it back. The third time the anointing of God came all over me and I started to shout the words, "Jesus is God." There are many who have trouble understanding that Jesus is God, but Hebrews says, *But in these last days He has spoken to us by his Son, whom He appointed heir of all things, and through whom He made the universe.* The Lord is telling us that He came down to earth to give us life and life more abundantly, and that if He gave His life as a ransom for us, we are to believe it. We can trust Him for everything concerning our lives.

He restated this teaching some years later as I was traveling in the mountains in North Carolina. I had been praying and fasting about a matter concerning my life and ministry. It was the third day. As I travailed in the spirit, suddenly the Holy Spirit spoke to me very precisely, "Jesus is God." This was repeated three times, and each time I responded with the same words.

But the last time I said it, it was as if the words were fire within me!

In order to bring this point to a close, let me tell you what happened. On my first trip to Israel, the Holy Spirit spoke these words very clearly: "I have an appointment with you in Israel." I thought He meant that I was to meet someone. Little did I know the appointment was with Him personally. As I traveled to Galilee, the Holy Spirit prompted me to spend the night on Beth Shan. Early in the morning, at 4:00 AM, I was awakened by words of fire written on the curtain in my room! They said *I am Alpha and Omega, besides me there is no other God.* This continued for several minutes. It was like Moses' experience with the burning bush. When the vision stopped, the whole room was illuminated. It was the glory of God, all over the room! After a few moments that very light entered my being.

---

1.   For faith cometh by hearing, and hearing by the Word of God. Romans 10:17

The room became dark. The light was within me! Then I started to see visions. The Holy Spirit spoke again. He told me to write everything I saw. Before the visions stopped, He said that, from that time forward, not only was I to evangelize, pastor, teach—and wash feet—but, in addition, He placed the burden of *Prophet* upon me.

This occurred April 10, 1978. Everything in that vision has come to pass.

But, back to the story. There in the mountains of North Carolina I realized that not even a leaf falls to the ground without His knowledge. He knew my situation. All I needed to do was to believe His word, for it was not just a word: it was the very Word of God that became flesh and dwelt amongst us. Oh the glory! The power of that revelation overtook me! I repented for my lack of faith, and as I did, He gave me a verse: *Then you will call, and the Lord will answer; you will cry for help, and He will say; Here am I.* The truth that the Living God was with me became real, and it has been from then until now. It is not I, but He, who speaks and does. He is God; He is in charge. He commands and it happens. He is Commander; I am servant. And yet, as Moses and Paul, I am His ambassador. And that makes all the difference.

Let me give you some examples.

In Mexico City early one morning the Holy Spirit prompted me to visit Lupe de Malo. I went immediately, and as I entered her home I found myself in the middle of a family crisis. Lupe's daughter, Alma, was expecting a baby. The father was in the US. He wanted nothing to do with Alma or the baby. I asked for the man's name and his telephone number, and told her that I would call to see what could be done. Then we started to pray. The Holy Spirit stopped me and said Alma needed to repent, truly repent, because, as a Christian, she should not have been in that situation. They were not married and had committed fornication. And worse, he was not even a Christian. Contrary to the Scriptures, she had *become one* with an unbeliever!

Alma did repent, and then the love of Jesus embraced her.

It was then that the Holy Spirit gave me a word. I told her the man was not coming back and that he was not going to be her husband because the Lord had someone else to marry her and become father to her child; and that this was to happen within 24 hours. Her family could hardly believe my words. My wife, too, was amazed when I told her. Again I went before the Lord in prayer and told Him that I was just echoing what the Holy Spirit had told me. My faith was based only on the Holy Spirit. I did not make it up.

The next morning Lupe called and, with great excitement, told the good news that her daughter's sweetheart from High School had come after I left and proposed marriage to her!

Now, several years later, Alma has a second child and is very happily serving the Lord.

On another occasion, a Brother in Mexico came to me for advice. He was deeply troubled. It so happened that he had just built a beautiful, two story home—on the wrong property! His own lot was next door to where he actually built the house. To make matters worse, the owner of that property was going to take title to his house according to the laws of the land. The brother was so upset that he intended to tear the house down rather than turn it over to the other man.

I told him to give me a day or so to pray, that I was sure the Holy Spirit would answer. A couple of days went by and the Holy Spirit told me exactly how it should be handled. He was to offer to buy the home and property (for a very reasonable amount) and to include his empty lot as part of the deal. I told him exactly the amount of money he was to offer. Within a few days the whole deal was taken care of to everyone's satisfaction.

Once, I was invited to speak at a church outside Mexico City. While preaching, the Holy Spirit stopped me. He said there was sin in the camp, meaning, in the Church. I stopped and told the congregation that I could not continue because there was sin in the Church, and that I was going to pray to see who was at fault. Then He spoke to me again and told me it was the Pastor. I looked straight at him and told him he needed to repent and step out of the pulpit until the Lord took care of the matter. He did not do it right away, but a few days later he did repent.

Another prophecy was about blood that would be spilled in the Falkland Islands due to a war that would erupt between England and Argentina. At the time of the prophecy there were no signs that such a thing could take place. However, it occurred some three weeks after I left Argentina.

These things happened because the word of God was spoken as I received it. The messages had no more to do with me than the Commandments did Moses. God is in control; we are but servants and messengers. Yet, while *Silver and gold have I none, such as I have* (a word from God) *give I thee. In the name of Jesus, rise up and walk.* And that is enough, for Jesus is God.

◆   ◆   ◆

Another lesson has to do with waiting upon the Lord. It is one of the most important lessons in His service, for those that learn to wait upon the Lord can soar like eagles. They catch air currents and rise high in the Spirit, as if the very wind itself. Getting to a higher altitude should be our aim, for once there, we can please the Lord, bear much fruit unto God, and perform works that remain for eternity. It was Jesus, Himself, who invited us to enter into His rest and take His yoke upon us. He said His yoke was easy and His burden light. I compare this picture spiritually to being able to mount up and rest while you are involved in God's service.

But many stay too close to the ground. There they must flap their wings continuously. There is no rest, and little fruit. One device that keeps you near the ground is the taking of burdens that do not belong to you. This causes discouragement "over weight" and keeps you from soaring in faith. When you enter into God's rest, you cease to struggle from the enemy-provoked worldly burdens; and it is then that you can soar like the eagle. Luis Capdevila, a well known preacher among the Spanish people in Florida, says, "I've learned to wait on the Lord because every time I see Carlos and ask him how is he doing, he always answers with the same words, 'Waiting on the Lord'." *But those who hope (wait) in the Lord will renew their strength. They will soar on wings like eagles; they will run and not grow weary, they will walk and not be faint.*

◆   ◆   ◆

Another lesson is that we must learn to blame ourselves, not others. From the beginning of time man has attempted to blame others to try to escape responsibility and get out of trouble. Adam blamed Eve, and Eve, the serpent. It is my belief that as long as you do this you will have no peace or freedom. The first thing the Holy Spirit pointed out to me the day I was born again was that I was the one at fault. And, today after so many years, the first thing that I do when things go wrong is to perform a spiritual check up, in order to make the necessary corrections. In the flesh we always are looking for the speck in our brother's eye, not the beam in our own. Just recently I was looking at my clown collection, and the Holy Spirit impressed me that many of us put on masks to conceal our own faces: in other words, to hide who we really are. There is a need in the body of Christ for honesty. If we want the power of the Church to be restored, we need to shed our masks and become open and honest with ourselves and with God, who already knows and sees us and the intentions of our hearts.

We also need to wash each others feet, especially those with whom we are having trouble. Many times I have heard people say, I do not like so and so, but I love them. That is being dishonest, for if we are going to be together in heaven, we need to get along in this world. The problem is that we are not willing to wash one another's feet. Pride stands in the way.

But God is love, and the ability to love is to be filled with God's love.

◆   ◆   ◆

There is a final point I'd like to share. The Bible says *Whatever has mastery of you, its slave you become.* In my ministry I meet many Christians. As I counsel them, it doesn't matter what they are trying to overcome, they just cannot get rid of the problem or temptation; and many succumb. You see, the real problem lies in the fact that *they* are trying, and as long as *they* are trying, they will never succeed. The answer is in surrendering (and staying surrendered) to the Holy Spirit. Many do not understand that as long as they are trying, they do not let the Holy Spirit work in their lives. When He is in control, no matter what comes along, the desire is no longer there, for the demons that were controlling the thoughts and flesh are gone; therefore you don't have to fight anymore.

For example, before I became a Christian, adultery was a problem (among others) in my life. But when Jesus came in to stay, not only did I receive salvation, but deliverance as well. The first demons to leave were adultery and fornication. I never had problems with them again.

I ministered to a large group of women in New Jersey many years ago. After the meeting I had a phone call from one of the ladies. Her husband was an alcoholic who never paid attention to her although she was very attractive. During the conversation she implied that she was interested in me. At first I started to rebuke her, but the Holy Spirit told me to be gentle, that she was hurt and in need of companionship, and saw in me what she wanted from her husband.

The first thing I did was to disarm her by asking her to forgive me, that in any way I had looked at her in a different manner besides being a sister in the Lord. That was just a way to let her know where I stood with the Lord. Later I was able to pray for her deliverance. She ended up with a saved husband and healed marriage.

You see, when Jesus sets you free, you are free indeed. You don't need to try to be good. You just need to live a surrendered life unto the Lord.

◆   ◆   ◆

And so, having considered these important lessons, let us return to the story.

Turning On Your Sensors

We receive salvation when we allow Jesus to come into our lives. That is just the beginning. But there is more. The Lord told His disciples to wait for the power from above. And that is what we must do, for we dare not presume to do God's work without His power. He said, "Tarry <u>until</u> you be endued with power from on high." He did not say, "Tarry until man tells you to go." He did not say, "Tarry until you send yourself." He said tarry <u>until</u> you receive power. Obedient disciples waited together in fasting and prayer and worship and loving Jesus until it was time, and then the Holy Ghost came upon them; and then they were endued with power and anointed for His work.

There is still more: He gives His disciples gifts of the Holy Spirit, teaches them to put on the armor of God, and requires them to walk in the fruit of the Spirit. Thus they are equipped to move in the Gospel of Salvation, according to His instructions. Obedience is a must in order to win battles and please Him. But, when done His way, the heavenly reward will be seeing souls touched by your life and hearing *Well done My faithful servant.*

Several years ago I saw a movie based on a story that happened in Turkey. Although the man was guilty of smuggling drugs, his sentence and treatment were inhumane. At the end he and another prisoner escaped. After the movie, the Holy Spirit said that the next time I went to another country I was to go to the prison and look for people in the same circumstance. I told the Lord that I was willing and available anytime He would call on me.

A week later I received a letter from Pastor Jose Galvez in Mexico City. He told me that he had just come back from Veracruz, and that Hugo, one of the elders in the church, had become the sub-director of the prison. He said the next time I came we could go and minister in the prison. Ten days later I arrived in Veracruz, and accompanied by Jose Galvez, went to see Hugo that evening. We had a long conversation about the prison situation. Hugo said that the next day he would get permission and we would be able to see for ourselves. I discovered there were several U.S. citizens there, including some women.

The next morning Hugo was waiting for us, along with a group of teenagers who were to sing and praise the Lord. Hugo told me that I was going to minister to the prisoners. I was surprised since he did not mention that the day before; but the Scriptures say we are to be ready in season and out of season. That makes me ready anytime.

Hugo introduced me as speaker in the first big cell (galera) he took us. I preached that there are more prisoners outside of prison than inside, the only difference was that some had been caught. I told them all are guilty in the eyes of the Lord, and that is the reason Jesus came. I ended up by letting them know they could be set free while in prison. When I gave the invitation, I asked them to raise their hands if they wanted to accept Jesus as Savior. All but one did. I thought that they had misunderstood, so I repeated the question, but with the same results! The Holy Spirit directed me to pray for each one individually, and as I knelt with them and they were accepting Jesus as their Savior, the teens were singing and playing worship songs.

Immediately afterward, Hugo hurried us to another galera. There, with a fresh anointing of the Holy Spirit, the same thing happened! Of about 50 inmates, 25 gave their lives to the Lord. This made some 40 total. Then we went to another galera. In it were 30 inmates. At the beginning, one prisoner was trying to cause trouble. As I began to speak he was hollering. Hugo started to take him to a confined area, but I told him that it was an evil spirit, and that all I needed to do was to use the name of Jesus. I bound that mocking spirit and it became very quiet. To no one's surprise, the first one to come forward to receive salvation was the man that the enemy was trying to use to stop the plan of salvation the Holy Spirit had prepared ahead of time.

Later, we were permitted to speak to the U.S. citizens. Four had been drug traffickers. The lady had been involved in an automobile accident. After they received salvation, we talked with and prayed for them.

That night Hugo told us that drug traffickers had offered him money to let them bring drugs into the jail. At that time he was going through a hard financial situation. He told of how alluring this was, but His faith in Jesus was stronger. He refused them. And the very next day an ex-prisoner (who had been released a month earlier) came to visit Hugo. He told him that, after his release, he had gone to his home town and dozens of people had been saved because of his testimony about finding Jesus in the prison in Veracruz after Hugo told him about salvation. He also reported that he had started a Church in his town, and ended by inviting Hugo to visit and preach there.

The Lord predestined us to be adopted as sons and daughters. All we need to do is to follow the direction of the Holy Spirit and be in tune with His will. As in the case of these prisoners, so in all matters of serving the Lord: obedience and timing are critical. I am very careful in this matter because I have made the mistake of moving before His time. I want to be like the Israelites when they left the bondage of Egypt. When the cloud moved, they moved. If it stayed, even for a long time, they stayed. So it is my goal. As the Holy Spirit moves, I move; if He doesn't, I don't.

Not long ago, we were on a bus for Guatemala City. As we traveled we came to where there was an accident on the road ahead. We were stuck for over an hour. The Holy Spirit reminded me of the subject I preached a week before in Mexico City. It had to do with making the most of the opportunities that He gives us. So I told Alejandra and the children to pray for the message, and I got up and started to tell the passengers on the bus about the plan of salvation that was available at that very moment. The Holy Spirit moved and we witnessed as several passengers asked Jesus into their hearts.

On one of our last trips, we were in a very small boat coming back from an island in Lake Titicaca in Peru. A terrible storm arose and lasted all the way back to the mainland (about three hours). It was winter and the water was very cold. There was no chance of survival if the boat capsized.

It was time to tell them about Jesus, His peace, and the power of the Holy Spirit. We prayed and then began to let them know that we were true believers. When Christians pray things happen. Carla, our daughter, who was 16 at the time, was filled with the Holy Spirit and began to speak with the authority of Jesus. My son, David, 12, and my wife, Alejandra, were praying in the spirit beside me. We could sense a revival taking place, and when we reached shore, we had a fellowship meeting in the home of one of the passengers.

I remember the first time I tried to go to Israel. I was in Madrid, Spain, purchasing tickets, but the Holy Spirit stopped me. He said it was not time. Then, on my way to England, He revealed to me that there was going to be a hijacking of the plane that I was going to take. I found out later that my connection in Athens, Greece, was the plane that the terrorist took to Entebbe, Africa. Later that year while I was at home, the Lord spoke again. He told me to get ready, for the moment for Israel had come. His timing is always perfect.

On another occasion we were out of food. The table was set with all the utensils and ice water, of course. As we always do before a meal, we sat down and started to thank the Lord for the food we were about to eat. Before I could say "Amen" there was a knock at the door. When I opened it, there was Mary Nelson, a precious sister, standing with two bags of groceries and a check. She told me that the Lord had told her to hurry up.

And I said, "Of course. I was about to say, 'Amen'."

I am reminded of Mary when she anointed Jesus before His burial. While others criticized her, Jesus commended her for her timing.

Always Ask Directions from the Holy Spirit

After the battle of Jericho, Joshua and the Elders felt very secure knowing that the Lord was with them, fighting their battles. But later, presumption got them into trouble, not for knowing that the Lord was with them, but for taking for granted the daily direction of the Holy Spirit. Since Ai was a small city, Joshua started to rely on the strength of his army and decided not to seek counsel from the Lord. A Christian is never to forget that we follow the Lord daily; and it is on a daily basis that we are to take up our cross and follow Him.

I was in Mexico City and was getting ready to return to the States when a group of brothers came to see me. They invited me to go to a church in a town several hundred miles away. They told me how big the building was, how many farmers attended, and how much my ministry was needed there. They felt that congregation needed to witness the power of God in its midst, and that it needed healings and deliverances. It seemed right to me. I was about to say, "Let's go," until one of the brothers said that that Church gave very generous love offerings. As soon as he said those words, I rejected going to that place. The next day, I took the airplane and returned home.

The very night that I arrived in Tampa I had a dream. In it, I saw a large church building where I was the speaker, and as I spoke the manifestation of the Holy Spirit was so great that everyone in the congregation was being set free from bondage, and healings and miracles were taking place, and many were receiving salvation. As I awoke, I could feel the presence of the Holy Spirit, and I asked the Lord what all of this was about? He said, "That is the Church that you did not visit!" I told the Lord, "Lord you know my heart. I will never be motivated to go anywhere for money." He spoke to me again and said, "I know that, and I know your heart. But you did not stop to pray and ask me about it; and the enemy knows that." I asked the Lord to forgive me, and within days I was back in Mexico City and on my way with the brethren to that Church.

Upon arrival, I could see that it was the same building I dreamed about. That night, as I started to minister I could feel that the enemy had the people bound with all kinds of deceit, from religious spirits to witchcraft and fornication. It took a long time for the message to break loose. I looked at the brethren and could tell that they understood the situation. They went into prayer. Their spiritual warfare cleared the way. Suddenly I leapt from the pulpit, which was quite high, and as I landed on the floor, the Holy Spirit made entrance. I received the word of knowledge and started to minister through it. People were falling in all directions without my touching them; others started to confess their sins; others, I told what their sins were. Demons started to scream out and leave as miracles took place. Everything was a carbon copy of the dream I had a few days before. The Holy Spirit was cleansing the temple. We stayed several days teaching and admonishing them to follow the Lord as true disciples. They did take a generous offering for us, but it didn't even cover the airfare. The rest, about half, the Lord supplied before I returned home.

And there was a similar situation. There was a time in Tampa when we were fellowshipping at Dallas Albritton's. It was already late, but suddenly, the Holy Spirit prompted me to walk a few blocks down to Bayshore Boulevard. I told everyone that I would be back later, and set out. Once there, I sat on a bench. While I was sitting there, the Lord spoke to me, "You know that I can bring them to you, right here!" I said, "Yes, Lord, I know you can." I thought He was talking about an upcoming trip to the Philippines. After several minutes, I decided to walk some more.

Little did I know that a plan of God was going to be manifested shortly.

About a block from where I had been sitting, a man came from the opposite direction. We crossed paths and I kept on walking. Immediately the Holy Spirit asked why I did not speak to him, for he was a homosexual. I told the Lord that if he would stop, I would go to him. Well, he did, exactly where I had been sitting. I went back and started a conversation. He admitted his unnatural desires. I told him that there was a solution in Christ Jesus and that he could receive deliverance right now. At first, he didn't know what to say. Then he started to cry. He told me that about an hour earlier he had been at a Christian convention in downtown Tampa seeking deliverance. But while he was there, a man stood up and told the audience that the only ones who never get deliverance are homosexuals.

After he heard those words, he left in hopeless despair. He decided to take a walk. He was suicidal. I told him that at the very time a man was saying those words, the Holy Spirit was bidding me to come to Bayshore Boulevard to meet him on a divine appointment. The Lord had heard his cry. He received deliverance right there without having to wait any longer. I remember, I gave him a hug, told him I would see him in heaven, and saw him no more. A few weeks later, I was sharing this story at the home of Harold and Joan Kent. Harold told me he had been at that meeting and heard the man's statement.

According to the Gospel of Mark, deliverance is to be a part of the signs that follow every believer. While some teach that signs and gifts are no longer in operation, I tell you, just take a walk in my shoes and you will find out differently. The Bible says *We wrestle not against flesh and blood, but against principalities and powers,* and we need the equipment of God to be able to do that.

As I already explained, when teaching the saints I emphasize the importance of waiting on the Lord. When you learn this, you can be in tune with the Holy Spirit and move in God's timing. Experiences in my life about this go on an on. And it is not just in my life, but more importantly, the Word of God is full of examples. Before Jesus called the twelve disciples, He spent the night with the Father. At the exact moment that Saul was going to have an encounter with the prophet, Samuel was there, even though Saul did not know that his life would be altered from that time forward. But Samuel knew, because the Lord told him. When the Lord appointed the next king, Samuel was there, for he was before the Lord in prayer. Elijah met Ahab at the property of Naboth because Elijah was in tune with the Holy Spirit.

We can go on with Biblical examples of how men and women of God stayed in tune with the Holy Spirit in order to bring to pass the word God spoke to them. And since Jesus is the same yesterday, today and forever, we, too, need to stay in tune. Let me give you a couple of additional examples.

Several years ago, I was preparing to leave for Mexico by car. The suitcases were already loaded. Within five minutes of my departure, the phone rang. It was Albert DeArpa, a prominent attorney in Tampa. Albert was known as a man of God. He was director of the Full Gospel Business Men's Fellowship in Tampa and publisher of *La Voz*, a Christian magazine published in Spanish. He told me that in two days they were going to Venezuela on a mission trip and that, at the last minute, one of the members could not go. He said that the Holy Spirit told him that I was to take his place. I told him I was about to leave on another mission trip, but to give me few minutes so I could pray about it. As I went before the Lord, the anointing fell, and the Lord said to go to Venezuela, that the other trip could wait. This put me in tune with the Holy Spirit. That trip made history, for not only did many come to the Lord for salvation, but they also received the Baptism in the Holy Spirit. Many still serve the Lord today. And not only that. But still, many years later, one couple who went, Rick and Beverly Crary, are still very close to our ministry. Even today, I still receive blessings from that trip. Albert, now with the Lord, wrote an article in *La Voz* about my testimony. It helped many people come to Jesus as Savior. And his wife, Marion, was a great blessing to our ministry for many years thereafter.

◆   ◆   ◆

An open door to the spiritual world.

Right after my conversion I realized as I read the Scriptures: something was missing; there was a lack of power and authority as I ministered to others. Then I read that, even after Jesus breathed on the disciples and told them to receive the Holy Spirit, He told them to wait for the promise that was yet to come. He told them to wait for power from on high, when the Holy Spirit would baptize them. They already knew something about this because, even from the beginning, they heard John the Baptist tell them that Jesus would baptize them with fire and the Holy Spirit.

The baptism in the Holy Spirit opens the door to the spiritual world. The letter to the Ephesians explains that our struggle is not against flesh and blood but against principalities in the spiritual world. In my experience I have come across different ways Christians have received the Baptism in the Holy Spirit, all with the manifestation of speaking in tongues. Which ever way they come, it is a wonderful experience. Here is my story.

Within months after being born again, as I was reading the Scriptures, a hunger for the infilling of the Holy Spirit came upon me. I decided I must have it. I told the Lord that if the disciples needed power in order to serve Him, so did I. They tarried, so I tarried; they fasted, so I fasted. At church I kept asking the ones that had received (there were a few of them) while others were still seeking. I recall asking a brother, Chancey, who was studying to become a chaplain in the military. He said he had being waiting more than five years. After hearing that, I went before the Lord and told Him I couldn't wait that long. So I continued in prayer and fasting. I was in the third day of the fast, when, at 4:00 AM at my beach cottage, the Holy Spirit swept over me. It happened over and over. I was crying tears of joy; it was unconditional love. Then I dreamed I was speaking in other tongues. But when I awoke, I was not.

Right after that Joanna Heard called. She asked about the experience. I told her everything. She knew that I needed someone with the gift of discernment to pray over me. She gave me the name of Bob Buess. She said she had already called him, and that he was waiting at his home for me. I went right away; and, as soon as I entered his house I could feel the presence of God. I told him about my experience. He told me that I had already received the infilling. He explained that the Holy Spirit was not going to take over and speak, but that He was going to use my tongue for the manifestation to take place. He asked me, in faith, to simply start talking in a language, and to not worry about the interpretation. He said the Lord would give the interpretation as needed. Sure enough, as soon as he laid hands on me I started to speak in tongues, and have not stopped since.

I went back to the church and spoke to brother Chancey. I told him the Baptism in the Holy Spirit was a gift from God and that he did not need to beg for it. The only requirement was a truthful heart. The next day I went to his home and, praise God, within 5 minutes he received the infilling.

From that time on, my ministry soared like the eagle. If I needed direction, I would pray in tongues and receive. It was no longer hit or miss. In the Spirit there was always a hit. In other words, the Holy Spirit led me to the ones destined for salvation; if it was a matter of deliverance, the Holy Spirit would reveal it to me. If it was a covered sin that needed to be confessed, praise The Lord, He would show me. I was able to say with Paul: I do not shadow box: I hit the mark.

The book of James says no man can tame the tongue. But, praise God, the Holy Spirit revealed that He can. Hallelujah! This last, rebellious member of our body can surrender wholly to Him. *God is a Spirit and we must worship Him in spirit and in truth.* For then, in the Spirit, we may be of value to Him, even as they were in the great example in Acts 13: *they were worshiping the Lord and fasting, the Holy Spirit spoke to them ...* and gave them the responsibility and anointing to take the Gospel to the Gentiles! Glory Hallelujah! As it was for them, so it can be for us. *Now the Lord is the Spirit, and where the Spirit of the Lord is, there is freedom.*

Revival

Jesus told Simon Peter, *Put out into the deep, and let down the nets for a catch.* Jesus had finished preaching to the multitudes from Peter's boat, and chose to bless Peter for its use. So He told him to cast the nets into the deep. Peter tried to correct the Lord, for he was a fisherman and knew that there were no fish. But he obeyed the Lord anyway, and once Peter obeyed, he caught so many fish that the nets were about to break. Peter knew it was a miracle. He was stricken with conviction about the state of his soul. Surely he had listened to the message Jesus spoke to the multitude, and was likely thinking about it himself. Peter knew that Jesus was a Holy man, and he, sinful. It was then that Jesus bade Peter follow, and from that moment, Peter became a fisher of men. He left his nets and followed Jesus.

This reminds me of the time that Elisha was plowing behind his twelve yoke of oxen and Elijah passed by and threw his cloak over him. From that moment, Elisha was never the same; he took a yoke of oxen, slaughtered them, used the wood from his plow to cook the oxen, made a feast for the people, and left to follow the prophet's call.

My *net* was my business, which happened to be a beauty salon. But the night I turned my life over to Jesus, I, too, recognized that I was a sinful man. And, like Peter, from that moment on I did not need my net to sustain me. That night, not only did I find salvation; I found life. The life that I was to live from then on was the life of Jesus in me. Just like the fisherman and plowman, my earthly income was no longer my priority. There was no turning back: like those before me, at once I left my nets and followed Him.

The result has been an adventure that, almost, cannot be described with words.

◆   ◆   ◆

It was a hot and humid day in May, 1995. Alejandra and I were very tired. We had traveled much of the day on a crowded bus on the way to Bislig City in Surigao Sur, Mindanao, Philippines. Then the bus broke down. We had just arrived in a small village and, at least, could get something cold to drink. We decided to make the most of the situation. So we joined the people in the village and proceeded to tell them the story of Jesus and His love. There were good results; some received the message with gladness. Soon thereafter, the bus was fixed and we continued our journey.

Finally, just as it was getting dark, we reached Bislig City. By that time I could hardly speak, for on the trip I developed a very sore throat. Pastor Erlinda Sorongon and her husband Tony were waiting for us with open arms and a loving welcome. We bathed and ate, and while at the dinner table Erlinda noticed I could hardly speak. They were expecting me to preach at the sunrise service the next morning. In a few strained words I told Erlinda that, by then, I would be able to preach.

That night as I lay in bed, I thought about how we had ended up in that part of the Philippines. While this was not my first trip to Mindanao, it was the first to this remote area. I had long since fallen in love with the friendly, loveable people of the Philippines, who may be the most hospitable on earth. They taught me many lessons about humility that have served me well.

My thoughts went back to the week before. We had been in Surigao Norte, at the home of Pastor Julieta Chua. While there, Julieta said she needed to go to Surigao Sur to arrange for a pastor from Manila to preach at a sunrise service there. No sooner did she say that than the Holy Spirit told me that I was the one to preach at Surigao Sur. I did not tell Julieta, only Alejandra, and we decided to keep this information to ourselves.

The next morning Julieta left for the outreach church in the South, and we went on to Villanueva, close to Cagayan de Oro City. While we were in Villanueva, the Holy Spirit woke me up early in the morning with the word *Mabuhay*. I didn't know what it meant, so I asked Pastor Tim Jumawid. He said that it meant *Long life*, *Alive* or *Hail* to whoever you are addressing.

On the way to Surigao Norte, while changing busses in Cebu, we met Julieta Chua on her way back from Bislig City. Julieta reported that the pastor from Manila could not make the sunrise service in Bislig City, and she told them she was going to ask us to take that pastor's place. Then I told her what the Holy Spirit said while I was in her home, and that we would be happy to go. There was no doubt in my mind that this was a *divine appointment.* It was certainly more than good fortune that we happened to be in Cebu changing buses at the same time that Julieta Chua was on her way back, with no way to contact us for at least two more weeks. I was certain that the Holy Spirit had us exactly where we were supposed to be. And with those thoughts, I fell asleep.

Early the next morning, about 4:30 A.M., off we went to the main plaza of the city on a bicycle taxi that had a top. Before the service started I was allowed to remain in the back seat of the *taxi* until the worship began. While I was waiting, the anointing of the Holy Spirit came upon me. I started to weep. As tears were running down my face all I could think was of the great sacrifice that Jesus, the Lamb of God, had suffered for me, and of His love for me. That morning my heart overflowed with love and gratitude to Him for His sacrifice and love.

There was not a trace of affliction in my throat or voice. I was perfectly healed and able to minister to the very large crowd that had come from many different villages and towns along the coast. I spoke on the Power of His Resurrection. The anointing of His Holy Spirit was all over me, and just as I was about to close the service, the Holy Spirit spoke to me very clearly the word *Mabuhay.* Then I realized what it was all about, and I said in a loud voice, over and over again:

Mabuhay, Jesus! Mabuhay, Jesus! Mabuhay, Jesus!

At this point everyone fell on their knees weeping and crying out: some in repentance; others asking for salvation; some for deliverance; and others for reconciliation and thanksgiving to Jesus for His great salvation. What all happened that morning, and the blessings that came afterwards, only heaven can tell, but this much I can say: Jesus is alive! Long live Jesus; Mabuhay, Jesus!

In my years I have seen the Lord do many special things. He is the source of and power for revival. But, it must always be done His way, and never according to devices directed by the flesh of man. Yet men persist in trying to tell Him what to do, when and how. Today, church organizations plan for revival, invite guest speakers, advertise in many ways, have good music, etc. They remind me of Gideon. The book of Judges tells an interesting story about Gideon. When the Spirit of the Lord came upon him, Gideon blew the trumpet and summoned Israel to fight the Midianites. Note that the Spirit of the Lord came upon Gideon; then, in the natural, he blew the trumpet and recruited a large army. This did not please the Lord. He said, *You have too many men for me to deliver Midian into their hands, in order that Israel my not boast against me that her own strength has saved her.* He started with an army of 32,000, but when the Lord finished, Gideon had 300.

This is how churches hold revivals. There is pride in denominations, pastors and leaders. They do it their way. They do not understand that revival is an act of the Holy Spirit and must be done His way. They lack the main course, which is prayer and emptying themselves before the Lord. To call for fasting and prayer—not only from the leaders but whole congregation as well—is out of the question. There are many excuses, especially from leaders. It was very different in the book of Acts. There we see that whenever the church needed to make an important decision, the apostles and elders called the church to participate, and together, they fasted and waited on the Holy Spirit.

And the difference is that the revivals I have experienced are still on-going. Souls are being added daily. What church? Not a denomination, but, Jesus' Church, the one He died for and is its Chief Cornerstone. Two years ago, my family and I went to Cochabamba, Bolivia. We found a lot of people there who were still involved in evangelism, with many being converted daily. The reason was that, over 30 years before, I was led of the Holy Spirit to go minister there for three days. Then about a year later after we had fasted and prayed, Pastor Agustin Enriquez went back to strengthen the brethren. When he arrived he found a continuing revival, just like in Acts. He simply watered the seeds that the Lord planted when I was there.

Many years ago I went to an island with the Pastor and leaders of the Church in Surigao Norte. It is located on the western side of Mindanao in the Philippines. When we arrived, the Holy Spirit fell. Today there are three or more churches, and souls are still receiving the Good News of the Gospel.

That is revival!

One of the most powerful and longest revivals I have seen has been in Cuatitlan, Izcalli, on the North side of Mexico City. Pastor Agustin Enriquez and three other families were led to start a Bible study and a prayer meeting in a home. Alejandra and I used to join them. I recall that, one time, the Holy Spirit gave me a vision of spiritual growth that was to take place there, and that from that work, a revival would reach out to other nations.

How would such a feat be accomplished? The answer is simple: by following the Bible. Agustin is one of eight Pastors. Seven others are under his leadership; but not really his, for Agustin is not the leader: the Holy Spirit is. They fast and pray together, and at times, have a 24-hour intercessory prayer team. Their teams feed the poor and widows and orphans; they visit prisoners and go to hospitals. They have over 300 cell groups. They are establishing churches in other communities and cites as well as other countries, like Cuba. Pastor Mario Flores and wife Enedina, minister in the city of Zumpango, Mexico; Jorge and Veronica Enriquez in Cuatitlan, Mexico; Horacio and Laura Munoz in the city of Tultepec, Mexico; Enrique and Dorita Mendes in Penitas, Mexico; Hector Salinas and his wife in Tepojaco, Mexico; and Fermin and Joyita who minister in Tepojaco.

When they started to minister in these areas, there were only a handful of believers. Now there are thousands of souls under their ministry. Every time we visit these churches the anointing of the Holy Spirit is so strong that people get deliverance and healing without even calling them out or laying hands on them. Their youth are being taught, not only by listening to the Word, but also by missionary work and ministering in the streets. They don't have time (or need) to be entertained; they are absorbed in the work of the Lord. And they are happy in it. Today, the flames of revival seen in the vision so long ago are still marvelously unfolding before our eyes.

Stories About the Great Provider

I would like to share a few touching stories where the Lord met people in their hour of desperation. These remind me of when the angel showed Hagar the pool of water when she and Abraham's son, Ishmael, were dying of thirst. The angel also promised that her son would live to become a great prince; and it happened exactly as she was told.

The first story happened in Mexico. As I walked into the hostel in Mexico City to see some family members who had just arrived from Cuba, I was introduced to a lady who was in anguish. I asked what was wrong, and if I could help. Between sobs, she told her sad story. She and her teenage son had been in Mexico City for a couple of weeks. They were waiting for her husband to come from New York with their visa to enter into the US. However, instead of bringing good news of filed papers, he said he was applying for divorce because he was living with another woman and could no longer support her and their son. After saying these words, he left. She was in desperate straits in another country with her son, no money, and no one to claim her for visa.

I told her that I knew someone who could solve her problem. Immediately, she thought I meant someone in the government or with a lot of influence. I told her that this person would top any expectations, and that He was more important than anyone in the government. His name was Jesus. At first, she did not know how to take me. Then I explained that she could become the daughter of the King *for as many as come to Him and believe in His name, He gives power to become sons and daughters*. I told her that she needed to forgive her husband and forget the meager crumbs she had received from him. In other words, she no longer needed him. She fell on her knees and gave her life to Jesus, with all its hurts. Bitterness, anguish and fear were lifted, and the burden disappeared. The next day, the same people who had seen her distress could not believe the way she looked. She was at peace and with a look of joy in her countenance. They asked, "Did your husband return? Did they call you for your visa? Did you receive money to sustain you?" To all these questions the answer was "No." But she went on to say that Jesus had come into her heart and life and she was sure that the Lord would take care of her and her son.

Three months later, I went to visit her and her son in Miami. They were very well taken care of without the need of her unfaithful husband. In this case, it was not the crumbs from her husband's table that provided for her needs; she was seated at the table with Jesus, eating of the bread of Life. He had taken her from the life of misery and desperation that her ex-husband had given her, and had lifted her up to sit at His table with Him.

◆   ◆   ◆

This next story is about a different kind of provision. It was like this: one day the Holy Spirit told me to fast and pray in the Spirit. Of course I obeyed, though, at the time, I didn't know why. You see, my job is to obey my Master, who doesn't always tell me why I am to do something; at least, not at first. After all, that is what faith and obedience are all about.

The next morning Francisco Pereira, a dear brother I had previously led to the Lord, stopped by to see me. He wanted us to go see a lady named Guillermina, so that we could proclaim to her the good news of the Gospel. Then I understood why the Holy Spirit had burdened me to fast and pray the day before. I needed to be ready for this mission.

We discovered, when we arrived at her house and talked with her, that she was a spiritist and a fortuneteller, not only in Tampa but in Miami as well, with many people under her counsel. Her house was dark and filled with instruments of idolatry and witchcraft. Darkness was everywhere. While I waited for a word of *knowledge*, I saw that she was limping when she sat down, and noted that one of her legs was several inches shorter than the other. Finally, the Holy Spirit showed me a son she had left in Cuba whom she dearly loved. Then my approach to her changed: no longer did I ask about salvation; instead, I asked if she would like to see her son again. That question changed everything. No wonder the Scripture says *Love never fails*.

The love of a mother for her child was touched. Her expression changed and she started to weep. Within few minutes she was asking Jesus into her life. Immediately the demons of hell moved in and she went into convulsions and was passing out. Francisco and I started to rebuke the demons and cast them out. The demon of epilepsy was strongest. It dominated those of death, witchcraft, and necromancy. Guillermina started to cry out that she was burning inside; her husband was very upset and started to bring her a glass of water, but I stopped him and told him that everything was going to be all right. Finally, all the demons came out shaking her body as they left.

Immediately, peace and calm came over her. I asked if she wanted to be healed now that the demons were gone. Guillermina told us that at a young age she had contracted polio, and that was why one leg was shorter than the other. She also told us that she got involved with spiritism after she had suffered several attacks of epilepsy. She used to call on certain spirits as she was taken into a séance to help her out of the epilepsy attack. Now that the light of Jesus had come to her life, she was ready for healing. We prayed for her leg to grow and it did. The miracle took place and the glory of the Lord filled her house. Now that her body had become the temple of the Holy Spirit, her house was swept clean as well. We took two full sacks of the instruments of witchcraft and idolatry out of her home and burned them. Her husband, who was very skeptical at first, later became a believer as well. Francisco gave Guillermina a Bible, and she wrote in it, "Today is the happiest day in my life."

In the passing years, Guillermina and her husband have gone home to heaven. But before that, she left a legacy of Christian believers. She told everyone whose fortune she used to tell, how wrong she was; and, in her new life as a believer, she led many souls to the knowledge of Jesus Christ.

◆   ◆   ◆

The next story is one of the great Love of our Heavenly Father. When I first met Carlos Almeida, he was already a powerful servant of the Lord. But there was a deep hurt in his life, in that there was a gulf between him and his natural father. After Carlos left Cuba as a small child, there was no communication between him and his father. Then through the years, the enemy had put a wedge between them. Even though from time to time, the Holy Spirit would touch Carlos concerning this matter, time went on with no resolution.

I sensed in my spirit that there was an urgent need to bring this issue to a close. I spoke to Carlos about it in the light of the Holy Spirit. Carlos' ministry was taking a turn to higher ground and the time was right for a reconciliation with his father. I also told him that the Holy Spirit was going to make a way for me to find his father on my next trip to Cuba. Since I knew this message was from the Holy Spirit, I knew He would provide me his father's address.

When in Cuba, it happened that one of my nieces had just gotten married, and her husband was a musician. The Holy Spirit quickened me to ask him if he knew Francisco Almeida. Francisco was a well known actor in Cuba. He told me that he did not know Francisco personally, but he knew someone who did, and that he would inquire about it for me. The next day, I had the information I needed. I waited on the Lord for the right time, and several days later, as I was coming back from a church service in Havana, the Holy Spirit said now was the time to get in touch with Francisco.

I went to the place where actors meet and encountered him there. At first, he did not believe that I knew his son, but within few minutes of explanation he had tears in his eyes. He introduced me to his wife, and when she found out why I was there, she started to cry. She told me that for a long time she had wanted her husband and son to come together. The anointing of the Holy Spirit fell, and I started to weep. I led her in a prayer asking Jesus to come into her life. After that, Francisco went to perform, for he had to sing and recite some poems. But before he did, he told the audience that he was deeply touched because, after many years he had just heard good news about his son.

On my return to Tampa, I could hardly wait to tell Carlos. At first, he couldn't believe it. But, after I told him his father was an eloquent speaker, he was not pleased. Carlos said that it was hard to understand, if his father was such a good communicator, why he had not reached out to his son all these years. I left it at that, but asked the Holy Spirit to remove the wedge that was between them.

The following day I received an email for Carlos from his father. I forwarded it, and from that moment, the healing started. A few months later another servant, Ross Montgomery, went to Cuba and watered some of the words God had already planted. By the time Carlos, himself, arrived, his dad had accepted Jesus as his Lord and Savior. Carlos was also able to lead others in the family to Jesus. Carlos told me that, the first few days they talked and cried a lot, and that, now, he felt like he had never left.

Carlos Almeida went to be with the Lord recently, but before he left this world he witnessed his brother Saul giving his life to Jesus as I led him in prayer. Thus, Carlos' prayer was answered, for he earnestly prayed that all of his family would be saved.

◆   ◆   ◆

And there is another touching story about how the Lord reached out to one of His hurting servants. Here's what happened, and while I am at it, let me clarify the matter of *foot washing*. As I see it, the Lord established foot washing as a symbol of true religion. It is a commandment, and we are to do as a sign of humility. Washing one another's feet is true religion, for it puts us in the place of serving one another. Remember the words of Jesus: *Whatever you did for one of the least of these brothers of mine you did for me.* It shows our love for Jesus by taking care of the needs of others.

Several years ago I had finished ministering in Orosco, Cuba. Just before we left the house where we were fellowshipping, a pastor came in. After talking for a little while, he decided suddenly that it was time for him to leave. As he started saying goodbye, the Holy Spirit told me to give him a BIG hug. I obeyed, and while I was hugging him, I felt the love of Jesus pouring into him; so I held him for few more seconds. Then I stood back and waited, for I knew something had taken place. I noticed, a few minutes later that he was no longer in a hurry to leave. Then he started to cry. He said he had never been hugged like that before, and that he felt the love of Christ filling him with compassion. He said he needed that hug because lately he had been very stressed and under persecution. But after that hug, the heavy burden lifted. As he said those words I was moved by the Holy Spirit to wash his feet, in recognition that I was in front of a true servant of God. One can only imagine how much this touch of love and obedience meant to that man of God. The Bible says *How beautiful are the feet that bring good news.*

◆   ◆   ◆

I remember some years back while I was visiting a couple in Metula, Israel, you could hear the sounds of artillery coming from Lebanon, trying to inflict casualties on the Jews. These beautiful saints were in harm's way as they carried the message of salvation and hope of our Lord and Savior via the Christian radio station "Voice of Hope." They risked their lives every day for the sake of the Gospel.

The Holy Spirit prompted me to wash their feet, and as I was doing so the anointing of the Holy Spirit came down on all of us and blessed us with that simple act of faith. I will never forget the tears of joy and peace that were shed that day.

Every time I come across trustworthy saints, I wash their feet.

◆   ◆   ◆

The God who sees ...

The next act of the Lord's mercy and provision took a different form. Yet, it was the Holy Spirit just the same. It has to do with the truth that *nothing hidden that will not be exposed.* The Word says that *what you do in secret will be exposed in the light.* In the case of king David, his sin was exposed on the rooftop for all to see. There are a lot of stories in the Bible about hidden sins, and we have encountered many ourselves. One of the most striking happened as follows.

Our ministry has taken us to many places where we have seen sin prevent healing, deliverance, and the abundant life promised in the Word of God. In one trip, Alejandra and I were in the Philippines in the city of Cabaddbaran, Mindanao. Someone asked us to pray for an elderly man who was very sick. His house was by the sea. It was a long walk. Once there, we had a worship service and then prayed for his healing. We waited for awhile to see if there was any manifestation of healing, but there was none. Finally, the pastor who was with us decided it was time to leave. But I told him there was a reason for us to be there, and that we needed to wait on the Lord for direction. So the pastor said we should get the guitars out and start singing again. I told him that this time it was a matter of waiting on the Lord, of just being quiet and waiting for a word of knowledge from the Holy Spirit; that the gifts of the Holy Spirit were given to the Church for such times as these.

Everyone in the house found a place to meditate and to pray silently before the Lord. After a few minutes the Holy Spirit showed me a large box about 4 feet wide and about 5 feet long; it was very old and dark on account of age. I got up and I asked my wife if the Holy Spirit had showed her anything? She said, yes, but first she asked me what the Holy Spirit had showed me. I told her the vision, and immediately she had a witness of what the Lord had shown her. She told me the box represented a homemade casket, and that many years ago, perhaps 30 years, this man had been part of a homicide. Although he was not the one that committed the crime, he helped cover it up by helping in the burial.

I asked the pastor to please interpret word for word what I was about to say. I then spoke the word of knowledge we had received. The man's eyes opened wide. He was astonished! He went on to tell us how it happened. It has been so long ago that he thought it did not matter. However, he came under conviction from the Holy Spirit and repented of his covered sin. We then prayed for him again. This time the Lord told me He was going to take him home, but before He did, He wanted him to be ready for his journey. Before we left the Philippines, the Lord took him.

I believe it doesn't matter if sin has been committed within hours or days or years. The Lord wants a clean vessel before going home.

In Search of Ananias

Remember, Ananias was the man the Lord sent to pray for Paul. In that sense, he was the first in a long chain of events in the spread of the Gospel to the Gentiles. But, sometimes I wonder who led Ananias to the knowledge of Jesus? Don't you? Well in heaven, all is recorded, so one day we just may know. But whoever it was, I am glad it happened because it set in motion unending events that continue even today.

I would like to talk about that chain as it pertains to me. Three months before I became a believer, I hung a painting I had finished in my place of business. It had a person kneeling with his face to the ground. Behind him, a city burned. He was at the crossroad of life, waiting to make a decision. Further down the road there was darkness and fire; but to the side, an oil lamp burned. Those who saw the painting were curious about its meaning. I explained that the man was running away from a city that would soon be destroyed. Its destruction would be followed by death and darkness, but, the oil lamp by the side of the road stood for Jesus. All the man needed to do was to reach out to the light in order to live and not die. Little did I know that I was the person in the painting.

Lift up your heads, O you gates; lift them up you ancient doors, that the King of glory may come in. Who is He, this King of glory? The Lord Almighty—He is the King of glory.

As I look back, many times I almost received Jesus into my heart. I wrote my brother Celso while he was living in Cuba and I in the US. I described the plan of salvation and told him that, although I was not yet born again, I would be soon. Yet, it was seven years before it happened. I remember going forward at a church service. How I wept; yet, still, I left without the assurance of salvation. Once, while I lived at the Y.M.C.A., there was a man of God named John Fox, who lived strictly to serve the Lord. John used to tell me the ways of the Lord, and my how I was touched by his testimony! I would cry; yet commitment from my heart wasn't there.

33

Today I think back on the wasted time in my life. But the Lord knows the intent of the heart as to whether we are sincere. He saw my anguish, and, just when I needed Him most, sent Joanna Heard into my life. She was a good customer at the beauty shop for years. Prior to my conversion she had an encounter with the Holy Spirit through Bob Buess, a minister of God's Word. Needless to say, her joy had to be shared, and I was one of the recipients of the good news: at just the right time!

I remember the day I called and told her I needed help; and how, there in the streets of Houston, she told me that I needed to ask Jesus into my heart. Once the Holy Spirit's light shined on me, I realized that even though I believed in Jesus, I did not know Him. That night as I looked into the sky, I told the Lord that I did not know Him, but that, if He was real, that I would follow Him the rest of my life. I got to my knees and Joanna led me into a prayer to ask Jesus into my heart, confessing my sins. A few moments later, she told me to talk to Jesus. I had never talked to Him prior to this, except for repetitious words that came from my head, not my heart. I was silent for a few seconds, and then, out of my heart, came the words: "Jesus, I am tired." No sooner had I said this than the power of God came upon me and delivered me from my sins and heavy burdens, for it was Jesus who said, *Come to me, all of you who are weary and burdened, and I will give you rest.* Those sins dropped out of my life once and for all. I knew, without a shadow of doubt, that if I died that moment, I was already accepted into his Kingdom. That night I slept in peace for the first time in my life. The first thing I did the following day was to ask for forgiveness from everyone I had hurt with my words or way of life.

And so I began to minister for the Lord. And it was in that ministration that I met Al West, who was a vital link in the chain that can be traced all the way back to Ananias. Although the light of Jesus only shined upon Al for a short period, he was a person the Lord used to bring many saints together. He was as a chain link of faith.

I met Al at an airport while on a journey to Haiti from Houston. It happened this way: my travel companion pointed out two men waiting to board the same flight we were taking. They seemed to be Christians, so I decided to speak to them. As I approached Al, I went before the Lord. The Holy Spirit confirmed that they were Spirit-filled Christians on a mission to Haiti. I asked them if they were and they said "Yes." From that moment we became close friends.

Since they were going the same direction as we, but only half as far, we traveled together, and then spent the night with them where they were to minister. This gave us plenty of time to exchange testimonies. It turned out that, later, Al became the editor of *Logos Magazine* in New Jersey. As a result of his work numerous souls were saved and blessed in many different ways. He was very instrumental in taking the Gospel to the Philippines. Later, in a visit to his home in New Jersey, I met Richard and Don Malechoc, who spearheaded *Logos Magazine.*

But, back to the story. As we left the next day, Al invited us, should the Lord lead, to visit him in Tampa. On our way back from Haiti we stopped in Orlando, and before we left, I felt that the Holy Spirit wanted us to spent time in Tampa. I asked the Lord for confirmation, saying when I called, it would be Al who answered the phone. He did, and we went to Tampa. Before I left on that trip, while praying about it, the Holy Spirit told me about two things that would take place. The first was that I would to meet someone who, not only was going to receive salvation, but also would become a minister of the Gospel; and the second, that the trip was going to change many things in my ministry. Both happened. I ended up moving to Tampa. It was amazing to see the opening of so many areas of ministry and to meet the many Christians that I would subsequently work beside, in a large part due to Al West.

Dallas Albritton was one of the first of the new people. I met Dallas when Al invited me to Tampa. Dal's hospitality, friendliness and faith were apparent in those first hours, as they are today, many years later. In fact, as I think back on those days, Dallas was an important link to meeting the next brother in the chain. What happened is that we had gone out to dinner one of those first evenings. We went to a certain restaurant, but, while we were still in the car in the parking lot, Dallas said that he felt that this was not the right place to eat that night. We prayed and waited on the Lord; then Dal named another restaurant. It was there that I experienced the fulfillment of the word the Lord spoke to me while in Houston preparing for the trip to Haiti, when He said I would meet a man who would be saved and would become a powerful witness for Jesus.

The story is this: while in Miami after returning from Haiti, the Lord gave me the name *Francisco Pereira*. But I couldn't locate it in the Miami phone book. So I journeyed on to Tampa. Then, that night we changed our minds about where we were going to eat. And guess who our waiter turned out to be: none other than *Francisco Pereira*. Is that not amazing?

What follows is a letter that Francisco sent me. It said,

> "Brother Carlos," (as I was reading I realized he was calling me "Brother". When I saw him last, he did not know the Lord Jesus Christ.) "After you left, I went home and told my wife about meeting you at the restaurant where I was your waiter. I told my wife that I couldn't understand that anybody could be so joyful. That stuck with me, for I did not believe that the kind of joy you were showing could be achieved. I told her about the prayer meeting at Dallas Albritton's on Tuesday night. She suggested that I take my son in case those people were off in their religion. So I did, and as it turned out, when I approached the entrance to his home I heard them praying, and even though I do not have knowledge of the English language, I knew they were speaking in an unknown language. I started to walk away, but Mr. Albritton spotted me through the glass door and called me back. So my son and I sat down. While they were explaining the Bible, and even though I did not completely under-stand what they were saying, something came over me. I started to cry and found myself asking for forgiveness and asking Jesus into my life, not only myself, but my son, as well, gave his life to Jesus."
>
> "Since that time my life has changed dramatically. I no longer gamble, which produced a large amount of debt in my life and family. With God's help I can see a very bright future ahead for me and my family. I started, with the help of Mr. Albritton and some other brothers like Al West, a Spanish prayer meeting in my home. This is something that Mr. West has been praying about for the Bay of the Holy Spirit. Now I am looking forward to meeting you again, if and when you come to visit Tampa, so I can tell you of all the wonderful things that God is doing with me and the rest of my family. I am looking for-ward to that opportunity and am thanking God for leading you into my life, a life that I never knew existed.
>
> Your brother in Christ Jesus. Francisco Pereira. August 8, 1978."

Francisco was, in fact, a powerful witness for the Lord Jesus for many years, until he was taken home to his eternal reward.

As the search for Ananias continues, there is another brother and faithful minister about whom I would like to write. As a former wrestler, I have always been attracted to the Olympics, especially the passing of the torch by runners from hand to hand. Knowing that they had run from great distances was always gripping to me, especially as the last runner enters the stadium and lights the main torch to start the events. I like to note that, once this torch is lit, it burns until the end. This reminds me of a far more important matter, the spiritual truth that as part of the living church of Jesus Christ, every time we witness for Jesus we, too, are passing the torch.

Jose Galvez from Mexico City, who is now in Heaven, was a most outstanding torch passer. I met Jose on a mission trip to Veracruz, Mexico. The brethren there had already talked to me about him and how he ministered the same faith that I did. I remember one day while I was preaching, he came in and sat down very quietly in the last row. As I looked, the Holy Spirit gave me the witness that he was the brother from Mexico City of good report. From that day on, we became very close. He invited me to minister to his congregation in Tlanepantla, on the outskirts of Mexico City. Eleven months later, to the day, I was there. I remember it well. The house was small, but there were over 200 people, many standing outside by the windows. The service started about 3:30 PM and finished at midnight. Many were saved; many received the Baptism in the Holy Spirit and spoke in other tongues. The anointing of the Spirit was so powerful that people were laying on top of each other at the altar. The next day, we had a water baptism and all those who were saved and filled with the Holy Spirit were baptized in water in the name of Jesus. It was glorious!

From that moment on, every time I went to Mexico City, I could see the saints growing not only in the Word of God but also in their witness. This went on for many years until the day that Jose Galvez went home with the Lord. Jose and I used to travel to Southern Mexico to minister. What I remember most about Jose was how he would pass the torch everywhere he went. He told me that the church in Mexico City was a place to gather the seeds and spread them out; that many churches came from that. As a matter of fact, it was there that I met Agustin Enriquez, who has become an apostle of faith in Mexico.

While Jose was in the field, his wife Eva Casillas took care of the congregation in Mexico City. Since she had a restaurant business on the side, she also fed part of the congregation and the poor, so that, not only were they were fed spiritually, but naturally as well. I have never seen such compassion for the poor as Eva had. The Lord also used Jose as a prophet. Once he wrote to tell me how the Lord was going to direct my ministry; and it happened as he said. Signs always followed as Jose passed on the torch. Once they took him to see a child who was dead. After Jose prayed, the child came back to life. Healing and deliverance were always present, which caught the eye of unbelievers and brought many to salvation. I remember the mother of a Dr. Calderon was a member of Jose's Church. Dr. Calderon used to burn her Bibles, and say that Christianity was a myth. He wanted nothing to do with it. Jose went to see him and invited him to church. Dr. Calderon went, and the manifestation of the Spirit was so great that, after seeing all the miracles—he could not deny them, because some who were healed were his patients—he, too, became a believer. I had the pleasure of baptizing Dr. Calderon in water. This man took hold of the torch and, following Jesus, became an outstanding Bible teacher.

Jose not only passed the torch, but he also sustained the torches of others with extra oil by giving them encouragement and love, and most of all the Word of God. I remember how the priest had to keep the torch burning 24 hours a day. Like the priests of the Old Testament, Jose ministered until the wee hours of the morning or in the heat of the day. It mattered not to him. Jose Galvez was a good example to follow to be ready for the Master's return.

I'd like to tell you about another part of that chain. Several years ago, I journeyed to Bolivia, South America. The Holy Spirit had put a burden in my heart about needs there concerning the Kingdom of God. I started the trip going through Central America, and was ministering along the way. Right before I reached Panama, early in the morning, the Holy Spirit woke me up. It concerned a brother back in the US that was dying of cancer. The Lord told me to go back and anoint him with oil. This seemed very strange, for I was on my way South and He was sending me North. I told Him that I would obey, but asked, "What about Bolivia?" He said, "Bolivia can wait." Needless to say, I did as I was told. I turned around and went back to the States.

It wasn't until thirteen years later that I actually made it to Bolivia, and yet, I was right on time. I had learned from the beginning of my conversion to always wait on the Lord, and, especially to move in His timing. You can have the message but not His timing, or you can have His timing and not the message. If you learn this lesson early in the ministry it will be of great value to you.

Here are the particulars that set the stage for that first trip to Bolivia. Prior to the trip I was visiting in Galveston, and while I was in the parking lot of a grocery store, I met Willy Payne, a prominent business man I had prayed for a year before because Joanna Heard (the lady that led me to Jesus) asked me to pray for him. He invited us to dinner the next day, and while at the table in one of the conversations, he and Vickie, his wife, told me about a couple of friends in Bolivia who needed prayer. I told them that one of these days I was going to Bolivia to fulfill a plan of God in my life.

Another year went by, and I was again in Galveston. By this time Willy and Vickie had become my friends. They told me that the couple that we had prayed for in Bolivia was back in the States and living in Galveston. The following night we met them at the Payne's home. They were Juan and Iris Hirmas, and their two children, John Paul and Christy. I told Juan that some day, as the Holy Spirit would direct, I would go to Bolivia.

According to Juan, I told him to come to see me the next morning at my beach cottage and we would cry together. He came the next day and the Holy Spirit took over. With deep conviction Juan gave his life over to Jesus. We both were crying for joy unto the Lord. Within an hour I had the privilege of baptizing him at the beach. Then the Holy Spirit allowed me to see a deep conflict between Juan and his father back in Bolivia. They were not even talking. I told him that he needed to make peace with his father as soon as possible. Right away he called his father, made peace, and told him about his faith in Jesus Christ. Within three months his dad went to be with the Lord.

Another year went by. Since the Holy Spirit was preparing for a trip to Argentina (this was to be my second trip there) and since the Holy Spirit did not lead me to Bolivia the first time, I thought that this might be the right time. I called Juan and told him about my plans for South America, and that, this time I was going to stop in Peru on my way to Argentina. I requested his family's address in Bolivia in case this was the time for me to go there. If so, I would look up his brother and sister.

It turned out that the timing was right. I went to Bolivia, and as a result the whole family gave their lives to Jesus. A new chapter in the book of Acts developed (true believers are continuing to add to the book of the Acts of the Apostles). That next year Pastor Agustin Enriquez went to Bolivia to fertilize and water the ground in order to bring more fruit into the Kingdom.

From all of this, Juan Hirmas became another Ananias, for not only did he embrace the calling, but he also became a faithful disciple of Jesus. He started a home Bible study, traveled abroad, not only to Bolivia but also to other countries in South America. He also went to Mexico and Israel, especially Bethlehem. He was used with power while ministering at Pan de Vida, Mexico City, and the people there still speak of his ministry.

Juan now enjoys his eternal dwelling among the saints that have preceded us. While ministering at his graveside, I could not get over the number of people who testified how he touched their lives. His ministry was fruitful. The word he planted into hundreds of souls had now reached thousands, with many coming to the knowledge of salvation. While I ministered at his graveside along with pastor Agustin Enriquez, the Holy Spirit directed my attention to Joanna (and John) Heard, who were present. Joanna was the vessel Jesus used to bring me to salvation. I looked at the many who were attending, and told them that Juan was in Heaven because the Holy Spirit had used me to witness to him, but that Joanna's (another Ananias) reward was even greater, for she led me to Jesus.

But far more important, if it had not been for the sacrifice Jesus made there would be no hope for mankind. To Jesus be all the glory! What a day it will be when we will lay our crowns at His feet.

After Twenty-Five Plus Years

It all started some time back. I received three closely spaced phone calls. The calls had in common that they were all seeds I had planted over twenty-five years before that had not only germinated, but had also fallen on good ground and had borne fruit a hundred fold.

Early one morning the phone rang. To my surprise it was from Hidalgo, Mexico, from Ramon Garcia, a pastor I had not seen for over thirty years. It happened that he had bumped into Agustin Enriques, from Pan de Vida in Izcalli, with whom I have been in close contact for many years. Ramon asked Agustin if he had seen me, and Agustin gave him my number. It was good to hear from Ramon after so many years. He asked if, the next time I was in Mexico, I would come and minister where he pastors. I told him that I would give him preeminence, and visit him first.

The following week I received a call from Rosario, Argentina, from Mirta and Ricardo Peralta, who had just come across others that also knew me and had been wanting to speak to me and invite me to come back and share the gospel with them again. After all, it has been over thirty years since I had ministered there.

Last, but not least, Beto Pinzon—who now lives with his family in Tampa, and has a Christian movement to reach the Spanish population in the Bay area—asked me to be of some help in this endeavor. You see, Beto was not a forgetter; he had been touched by my teaching over thirty years ago while living in Veracruz, and he still bears fruit today. He has moved to the Bay area to help among the Spanish population.

So, the following summer I kept my word and took my family to Hidalgo, Mexico. Everywhere we went there was revival: souls were added to the Kingdom; miracles took place; and healings and deliverances and gifts of the Holy Spirit were imparted. But what stood out most was that the seed planted over thirty years before had been productive. It had taken hold in good ground and was still producing fruit for the Kingdom. I saw the pastor's children fully engaged in the Lord's work, pastoring churches, two of whom I had baptized in Tlanepantla, Mexico at the young ages of 7 and 10. Seeing them in service for the Lord was very encouraging, and, as they shared with us their experiences and the things they learned as I ministered to them so many years ago, it was very encouraging to me and my family that our Christian labor is not in vain. Most of the things they shared I did not even remember. You see, when you minister to so many people, they remember what happened in their lives, but you have little or no recollection, especially after so many years.

As we were leaving they invited me to a camp meeting of all the churches we had visited. This event was going to take place a month later. I told Ramon that I would wait on the Lord to see if I was to go. After ministering at Pan de Vida I took my family home. Three days before their annual camp meeting the Holy Spirit woke me up, admonishing me to attend and be part of the ministry at the camp meeting. The next day the money came for the trip, and off I went. Agustin Enriquez accompanied me, and the results of that conference, I believe, will go on until the return of Jesus.

Then, at last, the day came to return to Argentina. As Alejandra and I arrived in Rosario after 23 years, we could feel a great sense of expectancy that linked back through so many years. I noted that the ones I ministered to so long ago had become servants of Jesus Christ and were now pastors serving the Lord in different churches. As at first, they were still very enthusiastic. What impressed me the most was that what I taught them then was still in effect, but with the advantage that the Holy Spirit has giving added insight and revelation. I also learned that after I left, my teaching became very popular in other churches as well.

As soon as I told pastor Ricardo and his wife Mirta that I was going to visit again, they spread the word of my return to Rosario. A good number of pastors and leaders came to hear what the Lord had been teaching me. As we were breaking bread, they told me how they had witnessed to the new believers about how the Holy Spirit moved with signs and wonders in those meetings so long ago. Now, many wanted to see for themselves. Others wanted more of the anointing and power of the Holy Spirit in their lives. So this was the challenge as I went to the Lord in prayer, since I did not want these people to be disappointed. Many had come a long way to hear what I had to say from the Lord; others had been praying for us since they heard we were coming.

As I went to the Lord in prayer, my prayers were that Jesus would get all the glory, for I was but His servant. I also prayed that the things that happened before would happen again by the same Holy Spirit power, for I am but a vessel for His glory, and have no power of my own for mankind. The brothers reminded me of prophesies I told them and how all of them had come to pass; the miracles and deliverances that took place; and how many souls had come to the knowledge of Jesus Christ. One of the prophecies was about the Falkland Islands and the war that was to come.

As I was getting ready to minister, I realized that I needed to keep the people's focus on the Holy Spirit and lifting Jesus high. Sure enough, as I did the Holy Spirit came down and people started to receive healings, deliverance, and salvation. There were also miracles. Alejandra and I ministered in different churches, but mostly in the home church of pastor Ricardo Peralta where we stayed. Ricardo is married to Mirta and they have two beautiful children, Melissa, 23, and Jonathan, 16.

We also ministered at Omar Jose's Church. It was good to be there again after so many years. When I left last time, Omar was a passionate young convert, and now he not only pastors a large congregation, but also has a Christian radio station that reaches all over the County of Rosario.

The Lord also had in the agenda ministry to a Catholic nursing home, where hundreds of elderly were hungry to hear the Word of the Lord. After I gave the Word, many asked Jesus into their hearts and received the gift of salvation. It was awesome to see how some received healing as they heard the word about forgiveness, and they where able by the Holy Spirit to forgive those in their family that had left them there to be forgotten. There is healing in forgiveness and they responded to that. Jesus showed me that to abort the elderly is just as bad as aborting a baby. There was a lot of personal ministry as well, it was on a one to one basis because the Holy Spirit had planned that intimate time to minister to their individual hurts and needs.

When the meeting was almost over, the Holy Spirit impressed me to go around laying hands and prophesying in tongues, and to let Alejandra do the interpreting. It was powerful and right on target. Many lives were touched and changed on account of this manifestation of the Holy Spirit. The time spent ministering to the pastors and leaders, and the teachings and words of prophecy, encouraged and strengthened the brethren greatly. After almost every service, the youth gathered around the kitchen to break bread and fellowship, and during this time they would pick my brain until 2:00 or 3:00 AM in the morning. These young people were hungry for the Word of God, and praise the Lord, we were available to them.

Another thing that touched our hearts was their willingness to serve us and to make sure we lacked nothing. Ricardo and Mirta shared with us the testimony that when we sent them our love offering (three months before we arrived) it was like a seed of faith that started a chain reaction of blessed events. They fixed the church and their house. The people volunteered time, talent, and money to repair the kitchen and two bedrooms, and to build a new bathroom. By the time we got there, they had finished the project. What was amazing, and really touching, was that not only had they saved money to give us a seed of faith for our ministry; in addition, as a church, they planned to continue to give to our ministry.

Then, the day when we were leaving, pastor Omar told us the same thing, about how the Holy Spirit had laid on his heart to support our ministry. It was a very warming experience for us to see this kind of harvest after so many years. God's Word will not return void.

To wrap up these recollections, it was after the Summer of 2006, that I received a call from Beto Pinzon. I hadn't heard from him for some time, even though he lives in Tampa. Beto invited me to a Christian concert to be held the following weekend in the area. I agreed to go, but the thing that caught my attention was that, once at the concert, when Beto introduce me to his friends, he would relate many of the things that had taken place over thirty years before in Veracruz. This was really interesting, and therefore, I made an appointment to see him, especially since his mother, Sofia Pinzon, was visiting him at the time.

During that meeting, as we started talking to them, I began to remember the water baptism we held at the beach where so many people, right after conversion, sealed their faith by receiving baptism. They shared things I did not know. Sofia told us about many, who after being touched by the Holy Spirit, had gone on to serve Jesus. She said one time she saw a demon leave the person who was being delivered and run out the front door. Truly there was revival going on, with miracles taking place; even a terminal heart condition was healed with a doctor's confirmation.

I always said that the acid test in the lives of newcomers is time, and once more I could see the test of time in which Jesus had kept them safe by the power of His Holy Spirit.

Giving back to the Lord

As Stan Skipper was concluding his address to a large group of men at Pan de Vida, Mexico City, something took place that shook my spirit as I was translating for him into Spanish. In a moment Stan's words pierced my heart. I had a glimpse of myself standing before the Lord. Stan was ministering about family values, and what we men would have to answer to the Lord concerning our loved ones. I asked Stan to wait, for the Holy Spirit was moving deep within our hearts. A sense of repentance fell on us. The next thing, we were weeping before the Lord.

Heavy on my heart were the words of Jesus asking me, "In what condition are you returning to Me the ones whose lives I entrusted to you?" Immediately, thoughts came to my mind about my wife and children. The Lord had handed her to me as a pure bride. What kind of an example had I been? Had I loved her as Christ loved the Church? Had I given myself for her? For me, love was not the question; but rather, my examples. Concerning my children, from the moment I saw them at birth and onward: it was not so much what I said to them, but rather, what my actions toward them had been. They knew more about me by what I had done than by what I had said.

I realized that the best I could give back to the Lord was not good enough, and that I needed help from the Holy Spirit. Left to myself, my best would be but a very poor part of what I should have accomplished. I knew immediately that the only real love I could give would be the love of God flowing though me. What He had given me in purity would have been returned as a tarnished, bad offering. With that revelation, I understood more clearly the imperative to be a good steward in every aspect of our lives. I was also very aware that to those to whom much has been given, much is required. And that I was especially accountable: first, because the Lord had given me much, including a wonderful wife and family; and second, as a teacher of the Word, I am held to a higher standard. Woe to me if I fail to live up to that which I teach.

As Stan's teaching took hold in our lives, quickened by the Holy Spirit, we closed the meeting with a fresh revelation of God's will for our hearts. Many homes benefited and were restored as a result of that ministry.

The Extra Mile

✦

(Matthew 5:41)

While in China, Agustin and I witnessed what an extra mile literally means. As we ministered in a village in the mountains, our interpreter told us that many of the worshippers walk five miles every Sunday to get to the service. She said we needed to finish by 3:00 PM so these believers could return to their villages before dark. In other words, these saints walked ten miles to attend church.

This certainly corresponds to the extra mile Jesus referred to.

That night back at the apartment of our host, I talked to Alejandra on the phone. I told her about the ten mile walk. We talked about what would happen in the US under such conditions. How many would show up for service? Perhaps this would be one way to find out who true worshippers really are. Would any be willing to make that kind of sacrifice?

We were touched by the witness of the Chinese believers for the Lord, where, in some areas they pay for faithfulness by imprisonment or death.

We met Lisa Samuelson, another sister whose life is an example of going the extra mile. Lisa works with prostitutes and leads them to Jesus. In such a hostile environment, not only does she give them the word of life, but she also finds doctors, shelter and work for them. As we prayed for her, the anointing came down as a flood from heaven as a witness to her. It was as if Jesus was saying: *Well done my faithful servant.*

While we were breaking bread after a regular church service, we met several young women from Central and South America that had the call for China. They left everything behind to go to the nations. In that group we also met a young man from Mexico. In fact, he was Agustin's neighbor. What a pleasant surprise for these brothers in Christ to meet once again, and that so very far from home! This young Mexican's testimony was very powerful to the underground church of China.

As we waited at the airport to leave, tears were running from my eyes as my thoughts went back to the words spoken by our hosts: they said our trip was an answer to their prayers, that for over two years they have been praying for us to come. They also said that, out of the many they had invited to minister with them, we were the only ones to answer the call.

What a pity.

On a personal note, that trip to China was the first trip I'd ever taken that came as a surprise. I did not plan it. It came upon me suddenly. Almost before I knew it I was on my way to answer the call. The Word of God tells us to be instant in season and out of season, and I am thankful to have been able to respond to that heavenly call as an answer to their prayers.

On that trip we left behind a good harvest, for many responded to the call of God, and many also received the Baptism in the Holy Spirit, and are ready for service.

But, you don't have to go to China to walk the extra mile. Last year I injured my back when I fell while climbing to my roof. It was so painful that, at first, I could hardly sleep. When Catherine Albritton, a dear sister who lives in Satellite Beach, heard about my problem, she made a special trip to Tampa in order to treat my back. Catherine is a trained and licensed massage therapist, who cared enough to go the extra mile for me.

As the epistle of James tells us, responding to the call to service and going beyond your limits is pleasing to the Lord.

Real Heroes

✦

Unknown to the world ...

My model for a hero is Jesus. There could never be another like Him, and like John the Baptist, I, too, am unworthy to even loosen the sandals on His feet. We can glimpse His majesty in the Bible, especially the New Testament; and, we can also learn about His nature by seeing it in the lives of true believers, those who deny themselves, take up their cross, and follow Him, for a fragrance of purity and holiness radiates from lives given to the service of Jesus and others.

I would like to tell you about a few such servants, for they are my earthly heroes. Some have gone to be with the Lord; others are still here, and I savor every moment of fellowship with them. In the natural, heroes are often the ones who save lives. But what about soldiers of Christ, many of whom have already given their lives or are in peril of death for the Gospel's sake? We read about martyrs and how they died for the Gospel of our Lord. But, if our thoughts are fixed on these past heroes, we might fail to see the ones in the present, who are around us every day.

It has been a privilege to know them. I would like to tell you about some who have meant much to me and have enriched my life by sharing theirs, nothing withheld. I'll introduce them as I met them, except I'll save the best for last, for therein will be the story of Alejandra, God's gift, my wife. I can hardly wait for you to meet her, for she is a special gem unto the Lord. Some of her story is in her own words, for I asked her to tell of the origins of her love for Jesus. I think you will be touched by her heart and her commitment to Jesus, the Son of God.

In my teens in Cuba I had several heroes. One was my uncle and Godfather. He spoke English fluently and was very likeable. What I liked best about him was that he loved sports. He taught me many things about baseball and boxing. He always took time to talk to me. But one day, when I went to see him, he was talking to my aunt. He was drunk and cursing her. I couldn't believe it. Needless to say, he was no longer my hero.

There were others in my early life, one, the uncle of one of my best friends in Cuba. We decided to have a baseball team, and since my friend's uncle was very knowledgeable, he became our coach. I purchased baseball shoes, a glove, and other items, but after two games he took me out and put in a boy of his same skin color. Until then I didn't know he was prejudiced against whites. That really hurt me. That day I went home and destroyed my new baseball shoes. It was a long time before I played baseball again. Until then I didn't know the meaning of prejudice. I never saw a difference between black and white, for my own grandmother, Cornelia, the daughter of an Ethiopian slave, was black. I never gave any thought to the difference in color.

As I grew, I noticed that each time I had a hero, it wasn't long until I was disappointed. But, my Dad was different. He was, and still is, my hero, even though he is in heaven now. One thing I remember most about him was that when there was a disagreement between us, he used to call me to his side—even when he was still upset. As I approached, he always gave me a hug and said, "You cannot stay angry with your dad who loves you." And with those words, ill will disappeared. And now I tell my children the same thing.

Another hero is my big brother Celso, who every time I got into trouble with bigger kids, would come to my rescue. Even now he is still the same—my big brother who always watches over my well being.

But once I became a Christian, I realized what real heroes are. While not perfect, they are on their way to perfection because they recognize their faults and mistakes and are being forgiven in the sincerity of their hearts. Al West was a forerunner, and, even though I mentioned him previously, it is my privilege to start with him. A perceptive man and skilled writer, Al cared deeply about people, especially the needy of the world. He touched many and brought them together in the love and service of Jesus.

Jamie Buckinham is another. I met him while visiting his home in Melbourne, Florida, with Al West. Jamie was a remarkable man. One of the things that attracted me to him was his sincerity. He was humble, meek and a very talented writer who handled the Word of God with precision. He wrote a column, "The Last Word" for *Logos International*. I am sure many lives were changed by his books. One, *Run Baby Run*, made him the number one writer in modern Christian literature. He was also an anointed speaker who used to tell it like it was, the good and the bad, mistakes and all. The thing that touched me most about Jamie was, once when I was going through an intense trial of faith, he took time to call, ask how I was doing, and tell me that he was praying for me. That really moved me, for he was a significant man of God with many important responsibilities; and yet, he took time to call and pray for me!

Jamie, now with the Lord, is still missed by many. It can be said of him (like Jesus of Nathaniel) … *a true Israelite, in whom there is nothing false.*

John Ford, although with the Lord for many years now, left a legacy of faith and integrity in the Body of Christ. He was always willing to minister to and help others. I remember one time when he came to fellowship in my home: I noticed him looking around the house. I wondered why, but didn't have to wait to long to find out. Within few days he came back with a new carpet for my living room, which he installed himself. I took John with me on a mission trip to Mexico—by this time he could not talk any more because he had a throat operation and had lost his voice. But that did not keep John from witnessing about Jesus. He would write and pray to communicate and preach. His love for Jesus and for the believers in Mexico still impacts them until this day.

I remember a time when John came to visit me: he was weeping because he had been rejected by men when he sought to go into full time ministry. He was criticized because they could not understand how he was going to minister if he was not able to speak. Still, John set his mind to follow the Lord all the way, but in the process, the Lord called him home.

I discovered that Paul Markowich had the gift of being a helper in Christian circles. Right after I met him, one night the lights at my house started going out one by one. There was a short in the meter box. As I was getting ready to call an electrician, Paul called to see how I was doing. Before I hung up the phone, the Holy Spirit told me to ask him if he knew a good electrician. He laughed, and told me that he was a master electrician, and among other things, was skilled in home improvements. Within minutes, he came to my home and fixed the problem. We became good friends. I took Paul on several mission trips, and the results were the same every where we went: not only did he minister by praying for the sick, but people found him to be a true Christian helper. When not ministering, I could find him painting a church building or working at Carlos Avelar's auto body shop. He would fix cars with Carlos and minister to everyone that came along.

I'd like to share a story about Paul. It was told by a brother who was trying to learn Spanish at the time. Paul used to joke with the brother and tell him the Lord was going to give him the Spanish language without study, because he had prayed and asked for it, and because he did not have time or talent to study it himself.

Well, here's what happened. Paul went with me on one of my trips to Mexico. When it was time for my return, he wanted to stay longer. So Paul, who could speak no Spanish, stayed with Agustin in Mexico City for another week. During the many services, Paul could be found in the back of the building praying in the Spirit for the preaching, singing and ministry that was going on up front. Then, at the conclusion of each service, he would go to the altar to pray for those in need.

It turned out that, on the last night of Paul's stay, Pastor Agustin was at the altar for prayer. Paul laid hands on Agustin, and praying in the tongues of men and angels, prayed a most perfect prayer—in Spanish! Paul didn't even know he was praying in Spanish until later when the brethren said: "We didn't know you could speak Spanish." Only then did Paul realize the Lord had answered his prayer and given him the *tongue* of perfect Spanish.

Paul passed into Heaven unexpectedly not long after that trip. He is a good brother that we all look forward to seeing again one Glorious Morning. At his memorial service, many people spoke of his service to the Lord.

John Zentmeyer was a man who couldn't stand to see anyone in need. He was always ready to help or to find out a way to pitch in. Once he saw that I needed a battery charger for my video camera. The next thing I knew he had made one. It was a small charger that could be used with different voltages and could also be plugged into a car lighter. The last time I saw John I was on my way to Mexico. He handed me a check for $400. What caught my attention was that the trip was already paid for in full, so I told him that the Lord had already provided all my expenses for that trip. But he said that the Holy Spirit told him to give it to me and that he was being obedient. I took the money and put it away. Little did I know that I was going to need it to make a quick trip back to Tampa a few days after I arrived in Mexico City because John was killed in an airplane accident on his way to Tallahassee. At his memorial service, a lot of people gave testimonies of how John was greatly used in their lives and how the seed that he planted was bearing fruit. A couple of years later, I went with his mother to see his graveside. Tears began to flow from my eyes as I thanked the Lord for the time I was allowed to spend in fellowship with him.

I believe Terry Jones learned much from the Apostle Paul, for he has been serving the Lord for many years while *making tents* like Paul did. In other words, Terry and his wife, Michelle, have been pastoring at Christ Center Fellowship for many years while working as writers. Many times I have seen them give from their own income to help people in need; and there were times they did this when they needed the money themselves. Agape love compelled them to be heroes.

The Nelsons, Gary and Mary, are true examples of what a Christian family ought to be. Each of their children must answer to Christianity for the example they have received from their parents. All the years I have know the Nelsons, I have seen their steadfastness in serving the Lord. On one on my many trips to Mexico I met a pastor giving his testimony about how he met the Lord. It so happened that he received a battery operated, short wave radio from Galcom International. As he listened to the Bible broadcast, he became a believer, and is now ministering in the mission field. It turns out that several years ago Gary Nelson and Harold Kent started a different kind of ministry: they sent battery operated, short wave radios out into the world through Galcom International, especially to places where people did not know how to read. As a result, many receive the word of God and, as in the case of this pastor, become faithful witnesses for Jesus Christ.

Vivian Mercado, a dear sister in the Philippines, left us with a legacy of meekness and humility. On one of our trips to Mindanao, we took her a radio cassette player. As we handed it to her, she fell on her knees crying in thanksgiving to the Lord for answering her prayers. Once I asked if she ever planned to be married? Her response stopped me in my tracks. She said she was married to Jesus, and that all she cared about was serving Him. I can testify that she always made sure that all our needs were met while we ministered in the Philippines. She never thought about herself, but always emptied herself for others. As she left this world, she left behind seeds of faith and hope for many to follow.

I could go on an on with my heroes, those who are examples of true Christianity, saints who have blessed me through the years. Harold and Betty Harrison, who, for over 30 years have not ceased to pray and support our ministry, are included. Their willingness to help at all times is remarkable. Many years ago, while I was going through severe trials, Harold called. He was very concerned and made himself available to be with me during those times. Such are the things that heroes do. I share with them, and many other faithful ones, the salvation of so many souls into the Kingdom.

A good many of my heroes are still active in the work of the Kingdom. While Juan Hirmas was with us, he and his wife, Iris, were a team that ministered in one accord in the Holy Spirit. After Juan went to be with the Lord, Iris continued in the ministry. She is a remarkable woman of faith. I have seen her ministering in Mexico, where thousands of people were blessed by her teaching. Iris now ministers in China.

My heroes are usually not noticed by the world. For example, not long ago we were breaking bread in the home of Dr. Eduardo and MariTere Pascual. Before we finished dinner there were at least 10 calls. You see, Dr. Pascual is a very well known heart specialist in the area (to me, the best, for he is a believer in Jesus Christ). He believes that people should be treated the way you want them to treat you, so he gives a lot of personal attention and prayer to his patients. He said that the calls do not stop even during the night, and that, not long ago he was saddened because one of his patients died though he had been warned to do something about his heart condition. He did not follow his instructions, and as a consequence, died.

Last, but certainly not least in the presentation of my heroes, is my beloved family. My daughter Carla once, when writing a school essay about heroes, wrote about me. I am glad that she sees me as her role model, but I would also like for her to know that she is a heroine of mine. So, likewise, are my wife and my other two children, David and Hefziba. All three are serving the Lord as the Holy Spirit leads: Carla, who is now 21, is already in the mission field. She is spending time in Mexico among the natives, and is also sharing the good news in Israel. When opportunity permits, we go together as a joyous team being directed by the Holy Spirit. I notice that when Alejandra ministers, people pay close attention and many souls have come into the saving knowledge of Jesus Christ. David, who plays for the Lord and helps with the ministry as we travel along, wrote me a note once. It said, "If you ever feel that no one loves you, look at me; I love you." Hefziba, the youngest, loves to help the poor in Mexico. Every night after her prayers and Bible devotions, before going to sleep, she comes to my bedside to give me butterfly kisses.

Others also comment about them. Teresa and Carlos Menendez recently said, after Carla had spent a long weekend with them, "Carla's visit to us was a great blessing. We were impressed as she shared her life with us." (Teresa was healed from breast cancer and is now helping other women cope with that situation). Every time I go to the school office my eyes go to the wall that displays student achievements. I see Carla's name for being junior and senior of the year.

We get similar comments about David and Hefziba. Yocel Alonso, a well known lawyer in the Houston area, is very influential to David. He took time to go to Mexico when we dedicated David to the Lord and became his God-Father. Always Yocel brings out how David excels in everything he does. At Christ Center Fellowship he joyously plays the piano each Sunday under the tutoring of Dennis McClendon. At school he received the freshman of the year award. David has taken up wrestling. His style is very similar to mine, even though he never saw me wrestle. Even in this, he follows my footsteps. At school, Hefziba received the Timothy Award for Christian Character. And, Gaylon and Bobbie Wilson always want Hefziba to visit them in Tennessee, and while there, to share her experiences about mission trips we take as a family.

Our society has turned from God and the ways He established for us. One of the main elements is that both father and mother are to influence the lives of their children. Children need both parents; that is the way the Lord set it up. Parents are not only to attend to the children's physical needs, but their spiritual needs as well. It is not only what we say, but how we live before them. And not only that, We are not just to be an example to them, but we are to listen to their needs and to understand them on their level. After all we were all children once and learned along the way. When there is as argument, the answer is to pray together. You must understand: prayer works!

We are to pass on the legacy of Jesus to our children and on to the next generation. The Word of God is very precise about this. It does not talk about bringing children into this world; rather, it talks about training them, and that means spending a lot of quality time with them. It is a good investment that will keep you from disappointments later in life. The Psalms say that *Sons are like arrows in the hands of a warrior.* As a warrior, you want your children to be those arrows that will make an impact and pierce the darkness of this world in the light of the Gospel of Jesus Christ.

Children reflect their parents. They are a living witness of what we have invested in them.

Now, finally, you get to meet Alejandra, who perfectly defines what a Christian woman ought to be. She is a Proverbs 31 wife. How I love, appreciate and esteem her. Her faithfulness and ministry to me and her love and service to my Lord Jesus are exemplary.

I asked Alejandra tell her story in her own words.

She said, "As long as I can remember I have always been in love with God. Though I grew up in a Catholic home, my parents were not very religious. But my mother had an aunt whose name was Cuca. I liked to visit aunt Cuca because every day she prayed the rosary several times, and also went to Mass. At home, church was not that important to my mother, so we only went to services once in a while. But I always loved to go, and when I took my first communion, felt very close to God. Even though I believed in God, and knew that He loved me, there was always doubt in my heart. I felt He was too busy—and I too insignificant—to listen to my prayers. I also thought that I was not good enough, and that when I died I would not make it to heaven. Maybe I felt that way because my parents divorced when I was six years old and my father moved out of the house. Those next six years were sad and painful because of my parents' mistakes. But the Scriptures say *But where sin increased, grace increased all the more.* God gave me His grace and love through my grandmother Teresa, my father's mother. My grandmother was not as religious as aunt Cuca, but she practiced in her life the two great commandments, to love God with all your heart, and your neighbor as your self."

"In 1979, during the Christmas season, my father let me visit Milka in Tijuana. I call her "Aunt" even though she is not a relative but a close friend. I was very excited about going to see her for I knew that she would take me to Disneyland. I always had a wonderful time with her family, but when I got there this time something was different. She had become a born-again Christian. I did not know that after she became a Christian she started praying for my family and me to be saved. As she witnessed to me about the Lord, the first thing I noticed was that Jesus was a real friend in her life; and, I knew that I didn't know Him that way. The more she talked, the more my heart was convicted of my sin. I knew that even though I believed in Him, I didn't know Him personally. So when my aunt asked me if I wanted to ask Jesus to come in to my heart, I was more than ready! I was almost thirteen years old when I was born again. I praise the Lord for saving me before my teenage years. I can only imagine the mistakes and bad choices I would have made without the fear of God in my heart."

"After I became a Christian, all I wanted to do was to tell my family and friends about Jesus. When I came back home, the first thing I told my mother was that she needed to repent and ask Jesus into her heart. I was shocked when she told me that I was crazy and I didn't know what I was talking about. I couldn't understand how people could reject the Lord. But as I started to read and study the Bible, I began to understand. My grandmother and my brother did accept the Lord, and the three of us began to fellowship in a Methodist Church. During the next three years I grew in the Word of God, although I had not been baptized in water or received the baptism of the Holy Spirit. It was not that I wasn't ready, but because the Methodist church we attended did not believe it was for now. However, one of the most important lessons that I learned during this time was to obey and honor my parents even though they were not Christians. Another good lesson I learned was to *Flee the evil desires of youth, and pursue righteousness, faith, love and peace, along with those who call on the Lord out of a pure heart.* The Lord gave me this verse very clearly one day as I was praying for the opportunity to witness to a boy that I really liked. But when I read it, the Lord told me clearly that I would be the last person He would use to witness to him. He showed me how the enemy uses this method to deceive Christians because, even though they are spiritually strong and have only the best intention to witness for the Lord, little by little passion takes control of the flesh; and then, the heart; and then, it is too late to run. That is why Paul instructed Timothy to flee—run as fast as you can—from youthful lust. I was obedient to the voice of the Holy Spirit, and I am sure, because of that, that I was spared a lot of pain and heartache."

"In Mexico, we start High School in the tenth grade. I was very excited about going and about all the new things that I was going to learn there. It was my second week when I met a Christian girl who invited me to come after class to a prayer meeting right there at school. I had a good witness to her in my spirit, and therefore immediately said "Yes." The presence of the Lord was so strong in that meeting that it was awesome. That day I met Agustin Enriquez since he was in charge of the group. Agustin preached about being baptized in water and about the baptism of the Holy Spirit. I was so convicted in my heart that as soon as he finished I told him that I wanted to be water baptized as soon as possible. Three days later I was water-baptized, and as soon as I came up from the river Agustin laid hands on me and prayed. Immediately I received the baptism of the Holy Spirit and started to speak in tongues. When I returned home, I was so on fire for Jesus that my parents thought I had gone crazy all over again."

"I am not sure that I have walked through the Kidron Valley, but I can said that I went through the fire when I fell in love with Carlos. I met him three months after I received the baptism of the Holy Spirit. And I will never forget the first time I heard him preach. The anointing of the Holy Spirit was so strong that every word he spoke was like fire in my heart. After he finished preaching he allowed the gifts of the Holy Spirit to be manifested and I saw and heard awesome things. For the next year and a half, I saw Carlos every time he came to Mexico. I remember praying that the man God had prepared to be my husband would be like Carlos. And, I was going to ask Carlos to marry us. Little did I know for what I was praying."

"I fell in love with Carlos when he took my hand as we were coming back from a prayer meeting. He didn't say anything; he just took my hand and when I look into his eyes I fell completely in love. When I got home and I realized what I was feeling, I started to rebuke the feelings in the name of Jesus, for I thought it was just my flesh or the enemy. But as time went on, I was falling more and more in love with Carlos (during the time he was not in Mexico). So I started to pray and fast and seek the Lord about what I was feeling. Finally the Lord spoke to my heart and he showed me that Carlos was the husband he had chosen for me. His words brought peace and joy to my heart, but the word of the Lord had to prove me true before we could get married. *Until the time that his word came to pass, the word of the Lord tested him.*"

"Being married to Carlos has certainly been a joy and an adventure. With him there is never a dull moment! In November 2005, Sara Enriquez, and a group from Pan de Vida, were going to Israel on a Messianic tour. The Lord impressed me to invite and encourage my dear friend and sister in the Lord, Maritere Pascual, to go with them. My daughter, Carla, now 21, was in Israel serving the Lord. Maritere invited her sister Yleana Newton to come along. Little did I know that, as I was inviting them, the Lord invited me to Israel too, and through them, He provided for me to go on this awesome trip."

"When I was in Israel in November, 2005, I learned much about our heritage in the Jewish culture. One day the Lord spoke to me as I was walking toward the Western Wall to pray. He gave me Ephesians 2:14 and said, 'Christians and Messianic Jews have to fall in love and stop trying to conquer one another.' And then the Holy Spirit showed me my marriage with Carlos. Even though we speak the same language, we are from very different cultures, but because we embraced our differences, we became one flesh and our children are rich with traditions and culture. I heard someone teaching on the Christian radio about the meaning of the word *university*. He said that university is made up of two words "unity" and "diversity" and that it means finding unity in our diversity. As Paul said, *His purpose was to create in himself one new man out of the two, thus making peace.*"

◆   ◆   ◆

And so you have heard from Alejandra. About her, I can only add, she is the Lord's rich blessing and crown to me in this life. I love her completely. The end of Proverbs says it best, *Give her of the fruit of her hands, and let her own works praise her in the gates.*

◆   ◆   ◆

As you see, these heroes in my life have touched me as I have traveled and ministered in villages and cities around the world. My heart bursts with affection as I think back to the life they so freely shared with me as together we look for that *holy city, New Jerusalem, coming down out of heaven from God, prepared as a bride adorned for her husband. And I heard a loud voice from heaven saying, "Behold, the tabernacle of God is with men, and He will dwell with them, and they shall be His people. God Himself will be with them and be their God. And God will wipe away every tear from their eyes; there shall be no more death, nor sorrow, nor crying. There shall be no more pain, for the former things have passed away ... The city had no need of the sun or of the moon to shine in it, for the glory of God illuminated it. The Lamb is its light.*

Oh the joy of our heavenly calling.

Pillars

And some are more than *just* my heroes. They are pillars in the church. Let me tell you about them. In the early 1970's two homes in Tampa were open to body ministry where the Spirit ministered at will. One was Dallas Albritton's; the other, Harold Kent's. At times there were Bible conferences between these two home meetings. I always note that the true test of Christianity is the acid test of time, and I have seen through many years how these two have continued in anointed ministry around the world.

Dallas was one of the first persons I met when Al West invited me to Tampa. In fact, I stayed in his home those first few days. He is a hero behind enemy lines who plays a big role in the warfare against principalities of this dark world. Dallas walks in authority and uses it when necessary, but he usually takes a back seat. However, the fruit of his work for the Lord reaches far. Many in the Philippines have been touched by his personal visits, prayers and financial support. As an attorney, Dal has helped many, not only with legal help, but also with the far more important matter of their eternal well being. I have seen him attend to the affluent and the needy with the same loving kindness; and many have come to eternal salvation through his ministry.

Dallas has been a continual nurturer of believers, and has been a mentor and teacher of many as they have come to know and serve the Lord. He has also, through the years, defended both *the faith* and the city. He has maintained a Saturday morning prayer meeting *for Tampa* for many, many years. And, through the years, Dallas has been a steadfast, loving, true friend to me. He has sustained me with food, shelter, money, friendship, prayer and love. What was his, he gladly shared with me. How I admire, appreciate and thank him.

Harold Kent is one of the true pioneers in the Charismatic movement. Many, indeed probably all, of the early seminars with charismatic speakers such as Derek Prince, Don Basham, and other bright lights who taught us so much in Tampa were arranged by Harold. All this was done quietly, behind the scenes, but he should be remembered forever for contributing so much to our collective educations. He was a personal friend of Derek Prince and he brought many other well-known speakers here.

The Lord gave the concept of the *GoYe Radio* to Harold. This little radio, powered by the sun, fix-tuned to a gospel station in the hearer's language, Harold looked for someone to make the little radio until he fell in with an Israeli who had designed such a radio but, finding no use for it, had thrown it in a drawer. Now they are manufactured, I expect mainly with Harold's money, and distributed around the world through Gary Nelson's group, Galcom. Untold thousands have come to the Lord through this faithful, obedient servant.

Harold and his wife, Joann, are a remarkable team handling the Word of God. One of the Kent's trips was to India where they have since ministered year by year, and where they are held in high esteem and regarded as Apostles of the Christian faith. Only in eternity will the many seeds of faith that they have planted be revealed; but the reports back have been awesome. Also while at home, Joann teaches the Word of God two times a week.

Glenn and Carol Allen live and minister out of Bartow, Florida. They minister in many different places in the world, yet, Glenn always makes time to participate in Agape Evangelistic Mission conferences and important meetings. They are always ready to serve the Lord. I refer to them as *gems in the desert* because Bartow is not a well-known city. It is but a small town in the middle of Florida; yet, these gems sparkle all over the Christian world.

Glenn teaches (and practices) that there are spiritual gates and walls that can be erected over a city (or nation) through intercessory prayer, worship and spiritual warfare. He feels that the Church has a role of *occupying* and thus defending the strategic place where the Lord puts *us*.

I would also like to mention Dr. W.S. Reed, the founder of the Christian Medical Foundation in the early 1970's in Tampa. Dr. Reed was very involved in prayer groups, especially those that focused on divine healing. He was a teacher and exhorter in the Church in Tampa. Dr. Reed wrote several books on healing and is still involved in getting other doctors to pray for their patients. Dr. Reed still ministers on Tuesdays here in Tampa. His has been a stirring testimony for many years in his city.

It is clear to me that Dallas, Harold, Glenn and Dr. Reed continue to be the salt of the earth. They are lights on the hill that cannot be hidden; they are men who stand in the Lord as pillars of good against the enemy in the spiritual realm.

Staying by the Supplies

From the very beginning, the Lord said He would take care of me and meet all my needs. And, He has always done it in answer to prayer, mine and others. There is no way that I would be where I am today without those who, so to speak, *stay by the baggage* in prayer and financial giving in support of my ministry. All of these help when directed by the Holy Spirit.

In telling this story, I do not judge others for asking for money to support their ministries; all I can say is that, in my case, it is a matter of personal obedience. I am to make my request known only to God; and I am to trust that He will supply my need. And, bless His holy name, He always has.

A long time ago I had the word from the Lord to buy a new car. I was directed to make a contract to make payments, and I obeyed. Shortly thereafter, Robert Shelley, Pastor of Bayshore United Methodist Church at the time, approached me to say that Bayshore was going to give $250 per month to meet the car payments. I told Bob that I needed some time to pray before answering, because at this time in my life money always came unexpectedly. After some time in prayer the Holy Spirit told me that this was from Him. He also gave me another sign. Harold and Betty Harrison, a couple from Alabama, told me that while they were praying, the Holy Spirit told them to send me an specific amount of money every month. I took this as a sign from the Lord.

Within six months the car was paid in full.

I decided to let Pastor Shelley know that the $250 Bayshore was sending was no longer needed because the car was paid off. Immediately the enemy told me not to report that the car was paid off, because if I did, they would no longer send me the money. But, the enemy's reasoning, as always, was a lie, for I had been told in the beginning that the money was for the car. So I went to see Bob and told him the truth. He laughed and told me that the payments for the car were just an excuse to give the help they had been wanting to give all along. He went on to say that they were going to increase the amount to $500. This continued for many years, and what a blessing it was.

But, as with all things, there were changes at Bayshore. When they decided to stop supporting my ministry, across the bay in Tarpon Springs the Lord spoke to Dr. Jim Gills concerning my work. Dr. Gills, in whose home I ministered from time to time in the fellowship that met there, felt that the Lord told him to send me precisely the same amount of money as I had been receiving from Bayshore. As a matter of fact, Dr. Gills asked Dallas Albritton about my ministry and whether Dal witnessed to the word he had received.

Dr. Gills and his wife, Heather, faithfully blessed my ministry for many years thereafter.

It has always been my prayer that only those listening to the Holy Spirit support my ministry, for then there is a unity of the Spirit. When I am on the mission field, not only do I benefit from the financial support, but I can also feel the power of their prayers. And just as they are to listen to the Holy Spirit, so, too, must I. More than once I have either return checks or asked people not to send any more, for the offerings had come with wrong motives.

I would like to list the faithful who have stood with me through the years, but to do so is to risk inadvertently omitting one or another. But, in truth, they all give as a matter of obedience to the Lord. None give to be recognized by men; and probably, most would prefer not to be mentioned by name anyway. Even so, my thanks go out to: Viki Payne, for her love, giving and kind words which touch my heart still today. She said, "I asked the Lord to give me good ground in order to sew my seed of faith. Jesus told me: 'Carlos is good ground.'" Rick and Beverly Crary, who not only contributed to my ministry, but more importantly, poured oil on my spiritual wounds. And they did not pour just a little. Rather, they poured and poured and poured until my wounds were totally healed. My debt to them is more than words can express. And there are Carlos and Leslie Almeida, who not only support our ministry, but also watch our children when we take short trips. And we thank Harold and Betty Harrison, for their many years of faithful support. I once told them that they were under no obligation to me, but Harold responded that that the obligation was to Jesus, for that was what the Lord told them to do. Harold and Joann Kent has been a special help for many years. Harold always seems to know when I am preparing for a trip, and always sends the right amount to help on the mission. Gary and Mary Nelson have sustained me through the years. Once they took me to buy a very good car. Gary explained that the Lord said I needed good transportation. Terry and Michel Jones and the brethren at Christ Center Fellowship have been supporting us with love, prayers and donations for many years. Somehow they know when there is something big that I need to pay for. Agustin and Sara Enriquez, even though they are burdened with the ministry at Pan de Vida, help support our ministry, for the Holy Spirit tells them when we need their loving contributions. I remember once Darell and Shirley Dyal gave their last money to the work. Dallas Albritton used to ask: "How is your money?" Since I would never tell him, he just started praying about it. The Lord would always reveal the right amount. Dal's son, Brian, not only supports our ministry, but is also a faithful servant of the Lord.

But, all that being said, it is the Lord who is the Faithful One. It is He who touches hearts to give or pray or love. Once as I showed videos of a trip to the Philippines to a dear sister, Carolina, she was gripped by seeing Virgie and her late husband, Tim Jumawid, feeding children in Villanueva, Philippines. Immediately after the video, Carolina talked with her husband, Orlando Cardona, and the next thing I knew they were contributing to the needs in the Philippines. In Merida, Mexico, Mary Sosa always takes us into her home for as long as we are there. Jorge Chan (and Lety, his wife) always stop their activities to make sure that we lack nothing as we minister. In Argentina, Ricardo and Mirta Peralta, put money aside for our ministry. Also, Omar Jose, uses proceeds from his radio programs to help us in the work. In Merida, Mexico, God used Javier Alonzo and his wife Griselda to start a chain of blessing for new converts in the region. I was honored to baptize this Alonso family. Today Javier Jr. is the youth pastor in a very prosperous church in Cancun, Mexico.

The list goes on and on, and the truth of the matter is that we are fellow workmen with these dear brethren, without whom our ministry would not survive. It is the Blessed Holy Spirit who has done all these things and put us together in the service of our Lord Jesus Christ.

As David returned in victory over the Amalekites, nothing was missing. Not a soul was lost, and there was much bounty. But some of his men urged him to not share with those who remained by the baggage. But instead, the king, the man after God's own heart, established a principle for all of time: *The ones who go into battle, and the ones who stay by the supplies, will all share alike. For it is God who gives the victory.* In God's Kingdom we share together in the harvest of the many wonderful souls that have entered into the eternal dwelling with Jesus and His saints.

But, in staying by the supplies, the most important factor is prayer, not money. When on mission trips, I feel the prayers of the saints whenever I am on the battle field helping to bring souls into the Kingdom. The effective, fervent prayer of the righteous are of much value. There are too many to mention individually, but these faithful brethren serve Jesus out of love. And theirs shall be crowns that will never perish.

I am thankful to be a fellow servant with them. Oh how I love these dear saints, pilgrims of whom the world is not worthy. The Lord knows that I thank each one from the bottom of my heart. And, you see, it is not money that is important: the Lord does not need our money; only our obedience.

Another angel, who had a golden censer, came and stood at the altar. He was given much incense to offer, with the prayers of all the saints, on the golden altar before the throne. The smoke of the incense, together with the prayers of the saints, went up before God from the angel's hand.

Agustin Enriquez

And then there is my dear brother and fellow laborer, Agustin Enriquez. I met Agustin when he was still a teenager, full of the Holy Spirit and with a zeal for the Lord. Through the years we have become very close in the ministry, and, under my nomination, he was ordained as a Minister of the Gospel of Jesus Christ by Agape Evangelistic Mission in Tampa in 1974. Now he is the senior pastor of a very large church in Pan de Vida, in Mexico City. In addition to this large congregation, which has some 400 home cell groups, there are four branch churches operating in other areas of Mexico, plus three affiliate churches in other countries, including in communist Cuba.

But it is not the number of churches or people on the rolls that distinguish this ministry; rather, it is the level of Biblical spirituality, the love for Jesus and for each other, and the joy in His service that sets it apart. For decades now the churches have thrived in continuous revival because of the move of the Holy Spirit through this humble and obedient servant.

And not only does Agustin spend his time fasting, praying and ministering in his own association, but he often makes missionary journeys to other countries, like the Philippines, Cuba, Bolivia, and most recently, China. For example, I remember the first time I went to Bolivia. The Lord opened a new chapter of real evangelism there. Within a year Agustin went and watered the Word that I had planted. A couple of years ago while we were there, we stopped to ask directions at a Christian station in Cochabamba. The man I asked directions from, when I told him who I was, said that the reason he is now a Christian is because a good many years ago, the ones that we led to the Lord, told him about Jesus. Tears came to my eyes as the Holy Spirit allowed me to see that, so many years after my first visit, the work was still growing, that my, and Agustin's, work in the Lord still remained. It reminds me of the fellowship Paul and Timothy shared in the Gospel. Paul ministered and wrote, and Timothy brought it unto full maturity. I believe that today we wouldn't have Paul's epistles if Timothy hadn't followed and watered the Word of God.

Perhaps in the early days Agustin was as a young Timothy to me. But today, he is a beloved fellow laborer. Always his ministry bears fruit, for he preaches Jesus Christ and Him crucified. He calls men everywhere to repent, believe in Jesus and be saved. He says *there is salvation in no one but Jesus, for there is no other name under heaven that has been given among men, by which we must be saved.* Agustin teaches that the Bible is to be studied, obeyed and taught to others, and that believers must be led by the Holy Spirit *for all who are led by the Spirit of God, these are the sons of God.* The churches under his oversight are full of good works and faithful ministry to the poor and needy, widows and orphans and those in prison. Saints under his oversight are full of joy in the Lord. They meet frequently in fellowship and breaking of bread, both the bread of heaven and of this earth.

Pan de Vida operates under a huge tent, where on Sundays there are so many people that they have to conduct several services. These believers take care of the community as well. They feed several thousand during the week. Agustin embraces fellow pastors, not only Mexicans, but those from around the World. He shares the pulpit with those who feed the Word of God to the congregation of the Lord Jesus Christ.

In regards to giving, I have seen him many times, filled with compassion for the ones to whom he ministered, open his own wallet and give the last penny all the money he had at the time. Also the congregation has learned from him how to give. Recently after a Sunday service they collected over $18,000 to help the Messianic Jews in Israel. In teaching the congregation to give, his motto is like the Bible: *freely you have received, freely give.* Presently, two congregations in Cuba are being fed by Pan de Vida.

Once, in Mindanao, Philippines, where Aley Gonzalez was pastoring, I was translating for Agustin from Spanish to English. The Holy Spirit spoke to me and told me not to translate, to just let him speak. As he spoke his English became perfect and the anointing fell on that place. A good many souls were healed, delivered and filled with the Holy Spirit of the Lord.

While some may ask, "Who is Agustin Enriquez?"—perhaps in jealousy or mockery, as Nabal of David—I tell you, he is a man of God. And I am delighted to call him my friend, my brother, and my fellow servant of the Lord Jesus Christ.

Carlos Alonso

Dallas Albritton asked me to write this book. And, thankful for such a faithful brother, I have. He also said that readers would want to know more about me than I might otherwise share, so, I have added this section. Hopefully it will provide personal information without distracting from Jesus.

It could be said of me that which was said of Joseph, "Here Comes that Dreamer." His brothers not only did not believe his dreams, but they wanted to do away with him altogether. This seems true for me also, not by my family, but by others. Like Joseph, the Lord gave me dreams and visions that have come to pass in my life. But, let me add a note of caution: individual prophesies, visions, and dreams from the Holy Spirit are conditional. They will be tested by time and circumstance, and they will require trustworthiness. Though our destiny was set a long ago, it is up to us to fulfill it. I say again, individual prophecies are conditional. Each person must persevere in faith until they come to pass.

Several years ago, I was in Havana, Cuba, ministering at my brother David's home, a lady came to visit me. She was an old acquaintance I had not seen for many years. She heard me talk about how the Lord was directing my footsteps and of the number of people who were coming to the Lord in different parts of the world. After hearing these things, then she told me that I had spoken to her about the Lord many years ago, when I was about 13 or 14 years old. What she said caught my attention. I asked her to please tell me exactly what I had said. She said that at that time I was very disappointed with the way religion was conducted, not only by the Catholics but Protestants as well, because they were not following the example of Jesus. I also told her that Jesus was not a religion but a way of living, and that someday I was going to start a system like the one Jesus taught. I was very surprised at her words, for I had no recollection of such a thing. But now, many years later, I was doing exactly what I had said to her in my childhood.

I recall as a young boy going to different embassies and travel agencies in Havana doing research about foreign countries, dreaming about going to those places, and wondering if I ever would be able to see them. Many years have passed, and there are but few countries that I have not visited since my conversion to Christianity. And, all this while since I've been ministering the Gospel, I have never mentioned a religion or denomination, for Jesus said *If I be lifted up, I will draw all men unto me.* This I believe and preach.

My friends say I am very tenacious. It is probably true, and it is not all bad. Luke 18 tells the story about a lady who wouldn't give up. She persevered with an unjust judge, who, though he did not fear God, yet because of her persistence, gave her what she requested. Jesus takes the analogy even further by telling us how much more our Heavenly Father will answer our petitions because we are His children. Over and over, time after time, I have gotten the answer I sought after spending as much time in prayer as it took. The Lord knows, and, I think, is pleased by the fact that I will continue knocking until He answers. And that is exactly what Jesus told us to do: to keep on asking, keep on seeking, and keep on knocking. He means, we ought to persevere and not give up.

In this vein, let me share a couple of funny things about myself. I always liked sports, and while in High School, started wrestling. Since I always liked contact sports, I pursued wrestling with gusto, but not knowledge. Years later, in Knoxville, Tennessee, I asked Bob Maher, a Christian wrestling coach to allow me to try. He told me that they were going to have a meet the following Friday. So, I wrestled in a real match for the first time. I had no knowledge of the rules or holds, but at first, using my strength, I was winning. However, after several minutes, I could not hold on, and my opponent beat me with more points. I remember going outside. It was snowing. I was sick inside, and said I would not wrestle any more. But the next day, I changed my mind. While it was not as easy as I thought, and strength was not sufficient of itself, nevertheless, I liked to wrestle. So I made up my mind to learn all about it, and go as far as I could. The first year I lost all my matches; the second, about half; but by the third, I was unbeatable. In fact, I became so skilled that I was able to represent the Cuban national wrestling team in the Olympics.

At another time, I wanted to build a cottage near the beach in Galveston, so I went for a building permit. Since I didn't know much about construction, I bought books on plumbing, electricity, etc. The building inspector did not think

I could build the cottage, so he kept asking me questions. But with each question, if I did not know the answer, I would open the books and find it. You might guess: I was very persistent. Finally, the electrical inspector overheard the discussion. He told the building inspector he might as well give me the permit because I was not going to stop until he did. At this he laughed and gave me the permit. Then he asked me why I was that way. I told him that before I was a believer I always tried to do my best when I made up my mind to do something, and that now, as a believer in Jesus, I was determined to do even better for Him. I witnessed to the man and he told me that he used to be an active Christian, but he had wandered away. I led him back to the Lord. Within a year I received a phone call from some of his buddies at work telling me that he had passed away, and that he wanted me to conduct his funeral service.

Months after I started ministering, the Holy Spirit started to teach me about deliverance. I met a young man named Rocky. He had only been saved for a couple of weeks. After a meeting he asked about deliverance. He said that he felt he needed it. I told him to give me some time to pray and wait on the Holy Spirit. Within two days the Holy Spirit told me it was time, so I rounded up some of those who were with me, and we started praying. At first nothing happened, but as we persisted the Holy Spirit told me to go for the main demon that was controlling the others. So, in the name of Jesus, I told the controlling demon and to speak his name. He did. It was Rebellion. I asked how many there were, and he said 21. It took about two hours to get them all out, but one by one as they revealed their names, they were cast out. In deliverance sometimes they come out right away; other times it takes perseverance.

Perseverance means that you don't quit, even when circumstances are unfavorable to you. In the Christian life, we have a champion of our faith who will stand by us until the end. *In this you greatly rejoice, though now for a little while you may have suffered grief in all kinds of trials. These have come so that the genuineness of your faith, being much more precious than gold that perishes, though it is tested by fire, may result in praise, glory and honor when Jesus Christ is revealed.*

I was born again June 21, 1968, and four months later received a vision from the Holy Spirit in which He called and ordained me to the ministry. Ten years later, April 10, 1978, while I was in Israel I was given the vision that my ministry had been sealed and confirmed. Since I testified of this vision in the front of the book, I will not repeat it here. But the fact is that God spoke to me in a very real and meaningful way, and I have not been the same since. What is required from us is faithfulness. I can, once again, almost hear the words I heard four months after being reborn: *Many are called, but few are chosen.* He chooses us by our love, devotion and faithfulness to Him.

Obedience is better than sacrifice. Right after my conversion, Joanna, who led me to the cross, called and asked if I had been water baptized. I told her that I was baptized as a child, but she said that that did not count in God's word, and to read it for myself. As I read about water baptism, conviction came into my heart. So, the same day I went to see Pastor Grundy, an ordained minister of the Pentecostal Church of God. He did not know me, but I chose him, because I wanted an organization that was as close as possible to Bible teachings. I went to his home, introduced myself and told him that I needed to be water baptized. He asked if I were a Christian? My answer was that, if not, I would not be there asking to be baptized. He asked me when I wanted to be baptized, and I said, "No later than today." So that night he baptized me. What joy to go under the water, leave the sinful nature behind, and be raised by that same Spirit that raised Jesus from the dead.

But I have gotten ahead of myself. Before service, comes emptying. And I confess that there were things I needed deliverance from and victory over. Anger was one of them. Anger is a spirit and if you pay attention to it, it will cause you to hate and a seed of bitterness will start to grow in your life until it will destroy you. The Bible speaks about being angry without sinning. When you start harboring hate in you heart, it will cause you to lose your peace, and eventually, it will affect your health. As a matter of fact, Jesus said that hate leads to murder. Your reaction to others as they deliberately or unknowingly hurt you, will decide your grade before the Lord.

I was born in Cuba in 1937, and there saw my Dad working many hours on the docks in Havana. He was paid good money, but worked hard. He saved his money and invested in real estate and in building homes and apartment buildings. As we grew older, we were able to enjoy middle class stature, but when the communists took over, he lost everything he had worked so hard for. I was the first in the family to leave the Island; and others followed later. During that time I had to pass on an opportunity of going to the world Olympics, even though I had earned the title of Wrestler of the Year and had participated in the Pan American games as a Cuban wrestler. The reason for my decision was that I would not represent a communist regime. Seven years later I was able to get my father and mother out of Cuba through Mexico. When I first saw my dad after seven years, he looked like 40 years had been added to his life. He came to the States and worked seven more years as a carpenter's helper before the Lord called him home. I loved my Dad, and seeing him work so hard after the communists took everything he had earned, hurt me more than anything I had ever lost or left behind.

I was filled with rage. I enlisted in a Cuban organization that was going to try to overthrow the communist government. I was very active along side my brother Celso while living in Houston. I hated communism and everything pertaining to it. Many times I ended up in fist fights when they held demonstrations. Communists were my enemies.

However, after I became a believer, the Lord delivered me of hate as well as many other sins in my life, and delivered me in such a way that I can now freely minister salvation to the communists. The change was profound. Here is what happened. Right after my conversion, while I was still working as a hair stylist at my beauty shop, I received a called from Joe Joiner, letting me know that the socialist party was going to have a meeting at a certain section of Houston. Joe used to call me to let me know of every socialistic event. I, in turn, would go disrupt the meeting. Normally I would call my brother Celso, and between both of us, we would attempt disrupt their event by yelling out, arguing and exposing their lies. The consequences of these disruptions were often fights, with a very high risk that someone would have been seriously injured. More than once I ended up in jail because of this illegal conduct.

But on this day, when Joe called, I told him that if I were to go, it would only be to tell the people about God's plan for their salvation. For a moment, Joe was speechless. He went on to ask what had happen to me. I told him that I was a born again Christian now, and my message to the world was Jesus and His love. Joe was noticeably touched, and asked if he could see me right away. Within an hour he was at the shop asking about what had happened. As I told him my story, he began to cry. He told me he had been a Christian, and at one time, had studied for the ministry. My words to him were, "Shame on you. I could have hurt someone very badly, and all the while, you had the knowledge of the goodness of God. Shame on you for not telling me about Jesus." Joe explained that he had backslidden and was no longer able to speak the truth. But, then and there, he got on his knees and asked Jesus for forgiveness and for a second opportunity to serve the Lord. And, as a matter of fact, from then on he started to take my mother to his regular church services.

But the anger in the family was not just mine. I remember once talking to my sister Conchita. I was witnessing to her about the saving knowledge of Jesus Christ, but there was something standing in the way. Finally the Holy Spirit revealed to me that she had hate in her heart. As it turns out, she too, hated the communist government in Cuba. It was deep-seated, but she found deliverance and peace in Christ Jesus as she let it go.

After the Lord delivered me from such anger, and through the years thereafter, I have met several pastors in Cuba who had been deceived by communism. But, because of the grace of God working in my life, I was able to love them, and because of that, was able to led many to the knowledge of Jesus Christ. And, because of this, they are now serving the Lord.

Anger and hate come in many different ways. Often what triggers hate is when someone close to you hurts you or has been hurt, like a spouse when there is adultery involved, or where money is involved. It blinds the eyes of entire families, who are sometimes destroyed. Forgiveness is the cure for hate and anger. Forgetting it might take longer, but, once you truly forgive (as you also hope to be forgiven) you will no longer be hurt as thoughts comes back to you, or as the enemy projects them into your mind. The fact is, Jesus overcame the world, and as a result, the power of the Gospel liberates the soul. I have seen many people on their deathbeds completely healed as the Holy Spirit revealed bitterness, anger, or hate in their lives, as they confessed unforgiveness and turned their lives over in surrender to the Lord Jesus Christ.

◆　　　◆　　　◆

I'd like to relay a few more of the lessons the Lord taught me. One has to do with compassion. We were traveling to Mexico, just before we got to Laredo, Texas, I had such a terrible backache that I had to lay down in the back seat. The pain was excruciating. I couldn't sit up. I did not understand. It had started two weeks before this trip, and yet, my prayers for healing were not yet manifested. Passing through Houston, I went to see a friend who was a doctor. He gave me pills to ease the pain and relax the muscles in my back. I accepted them, but didn't take one right away. You see, from the time since Jesus had become my Lord and Savior until that very moment, I had walked in divine healing, and up to that time, whatever ailment came upon me, I was able to pray it away. But not this time. The pain would not leave, and I was in that predicament.

Finally, I took the pills, but as soon as did, I started to cry before the Lord and asked Him, "Why, Lord?" Since I had become a Christian, Jesus had always healed me when I prayed. It didn't take long for the answer to come. The word of the Lord came to me in Rema, and said very clearly, "Carlos, you used to be more compassionate." Those words pierced my heart. As I recounted my actions, I noted how, lately, I was judging people when their faith was not up to mine. I was hard on them, and instead of showing patience and love, what they got from me were rebukes. I cried some more before the Lord, but this time with a repentant heart. When I stopped, I asked the Lord to heal me. He spoke once more and said, "When you get to Mexico City, I will heal you."

With those words, I went to Mexico City. The following day a Christian brother, Chucho Velez, saw that I was moving very slowly, and asked what was wrong. I told him that my back hurt. He told me that his mother-in-law was a good massage therapist and that I should let her attend to my back. He gave me her address, and I went to see her. It so happened that when I arrived at her home, she was not there. But I was allowed to wait for her. While waiting, I felt an evil presence in the place. The room was semi-dark and there were signs of spiritism and witchcraft all around. I discerned that the lady I was to meet and allow to give me a therapeutic massage was dealing with the occult. In a moment I made up my mind and said aloud, "Even if I remain with back pain the rest of my life, I will not let this woman put her hands on me." I immediately left her apartment. The next morning, while having breakfast, I realized that I had no pain at all; I had been healed.

I learned at that time, that even though the Lord had spoken to me, the enemy was trying to trap me before I received my healing. When the Lord speaks, He always keeps His word. We need to obey His word and guard it at all costs.

But the most important lesson I learned was not to judge others according to the measure of faith that I have.

♦   ♦   ♦

And there was the time the Lord re-taught me about the value of a soul. I had moved from Tampa back to Houston, so I sold the house. There was a window A/C unit that the new owners wanted me to leave. So I gave them a price and they agreed. It was $600. They offered half the money in cash and a funded check for the rest in two weeks. After I had been in Houston for more than two weeks I deposited the check in my account. To my disappointment it came back, not for lack of funds, but because it was designated "stop-payment."

This upset me very much. I tried to contact the people, but to no avail. So, I decided to pay them a visit the next time I went to Tampa. That time came and I went to their home. As soon as they saw who was knocking, not only they did not open the door, but they closed the curtains as well. By this time, I wasn't knocking: I was banging on the door and shouting. Finally, I told them I was going to contact the authorities and collect that check. I yelled, "I'll see you in court," and drove away very angry.

After I had driven about 3 miles, the Holy Spirit asked, "Carlos, how much is a soul worth?" I could not answer at first, for I knew my actions were wrong. So I started to cry and ask the Lord to forgive me. I remembered all the trips I had taken abroad to reach the lost, and the money that was used for that travel. But now, to my embarrassment, I was upset and angry about a few dollars. I was giving such a bad testimony of the love of Jesus. The Holy Spirit told me to go back and ask for forgiveness, and to tell them to forget the money they owed me. So I went back, and this time I knocked very softly and asked them to please open the door. They did, and I asked them to forgive me; and I tore the check into pieces. Then I told them that the reason I had returned was that the Lord laid on my heart the wrongness of my actions. As I talked to them, the Holy Spirit fell on that home and the family gave their hearts to Jesus.

Needless to say, the lesson I learned that day stayed in my heart forever. The price Jesus paid for our salvation was without measure. No amount of money could pay; it would never be enough. Salvation is a gift from God that Jesus paid for with His own precious blood. Just because it is a gift does not mean it is cheap. I wrote on my business card this message, "I asked Jesus, 'How much do you love me?' And He said, 'This much' … then opened His arms and died."

◆   ◆   ◆

Being an eyewitness is important to any investigation, and it becomes a very decided element in courts as they make decisions. In the four Gospels we can see clearly that Jesus' disciples were conclusive witnesses not only of His ministry, but what is more important, of His resurrection. When the disciples prayed about choosing another to take the place of Judas Iscariot, they wanted one who was an eye witness as well as a follower of Jesus. As they cast lots they prayed *For one of these must become a witness with us of His resurrection.*

In the Lord's ministry through me, miracles have followed the preaching of His Word, for signs should follow every believer. People are to receive not only salvation, but also deliverance and healing. The gifts of the Holy Spirit should be in operation in the life of every believer. The signs in themselves will be a confrontation to unbelievers, for even if they denied the faith, they still have to face the fact that they were eyewitnesses to the power of God ... *for the Kingdom of God is not a matter of talk, but of power.* Paul said, *My message and my preaching were not with wise and persuasive words, but with a demonstration of the Spirit's power, so that your faith might not rest on men's wisdom, but on God's power.* Pastor Tim Jumawid said there were a lot of skeptics as I preached on healing and deliverance on my first trip to the Philippines. But then, a crippled man came forward. When he began to walk (after the prayer of faith) they decided that Jesus was real. Many turned their lives over to Him for salvation. They became eyewitnesses and believers. And, out of that miracle, Tim, who is now with the Lord (having died trying to help people escape from a burning ferry a few years ago), decided to put into practice the healing power of Jesus, and many souls came to receive divine healing because he did.

It is what Jesus said: *Believe me when I say that I am in the Father and the Father is in me; at least believe on the evidence of the miracles themselves.*

◆   ◆   ◆

As time goes by I am able to see more and more of God's provision for His children. It seems that the longer I serve him, the more aware I am that He delights in taking care of His own, especially those who serve Him.

Once I heard an evangelist speak on faith, and how he lived by faith. As it turned out, after the meeting we had dinner together, and in the conversation he asked me about my ministry. When I got through explaining how the Lord always provides, and that I did not send newsletters asking for donations, he could hardly believe it. He went on to tell me that if he were to do it that way, he would not be able stay in the ministry for long. I was surprised, especially after he had spoken on faith, and I asked him why he did not believe what he preaches. He could not answer.

On another occasion I met a different minister. All he did was ask for support. I asked him why he kept asking people for money for his ministry. He said that it was the way he interpreted the Bible. Jesus said to ask and you shall receive. I told him it meant to ask the Lord, not everyone he came across. I also told him that his trust was in man, not God. Then I told him how, when I started the ministry, the first thing that Jesus asked of me was for me to feed His people with the Word of God. If I did that, He said He would take care of me. But, He told me to never ask for provision because He was my provider.

Many years have gone by, and it always amazes me how He provides for my needs from different people in different places as He bids them help the ministry. For example, if there is a month that I am taking a long trip, extra money will come in. If there is a month that there is no trip, the income will be for that month only. Sometimes it does not come as money. Needs are also met in other ways. Once while I was still a beautician, I was in the process of having a shop finished. Before I had someone build the driveway, I put in the culvert at the entrance. When the inspector came, he told me that the culverts were too high. In other words, I needed to lower them. As I went to prayer, two things bothered me: one, I did not have money to re-do what I had done; and two, the pillars were deep in the ground. If it took such a great effort for me to place them there, there was no way I could pull them out and put them back again. I earnestly prayed, and before I was through, I heard a rumble outside. Then there was a knock at the door. The man outside was a contractor who was going to put in culverts a block away. He needed a place to park his machines, and since I had such a big space, he asked if I would give him permission to park on my property. I told him to be my guest. Several days later, he came and told me that he thought the building inspector would not permit the culvert that I had placed at the entrance of my driveway. He offered, after he finished working in the area, to re-do what I had done at no charge, as his thanks for my helping him. He did the job within hours. At that time I did not have the money, but the Lord provided what I needed.

Later we met Richard and Amy Hague, wonderful Christians in Treasure Island, Florida. Richard was a delegate for the Full Gospel International chapter where I spoke on different occasions. We became fast friends and shared good fellowship together. Many times we stayed at their motel in fellowship and breaking bread together. Often they would move us from room to room as tourists started their vacations. They were able to bless us and still not lose business. And yet, they never charged us for our rooms. You see, it is not always money that you need.

Through the years, between assignments from the Lord, I have steadily worked on renovating our home. Our friends, the Dyal's, say I am like an artist and our home the canvas. They say that the picture is always getting better. At any given time, if you visit us, you might find me in the middle of a new project. And so it was on one occasion when my next project was to put tile on the bathroom and closet floors. But this was interrupted by a call for ministry at the home of Donald and Joan Jones. We were there for a considerable time (with Craig and Rainney Yaras and Danilo and Maria Claveria). But as that ministry finished, Donald asked me to come by his place of business to see the different tiles that he had. When I did, I found a style I really liked. As I started to pay, Donald stopped me, saying the Lord told him it was a gift. It turned out that for some time the Jones's had been wanting to do something for us, and this was their opportunity to bless.

When my daughter Carla turned 15, we celebrated her birthday in Mexico. I went to see Juan Medina, the owner of a large salon for festivities. We had a list of things we needed besides just renting the place, things like tables, refreshments, waiters, etc. I asked Juan for the bill, but he answered, "You owe me nothing. For a long time I have been looking for an opportunity to bless you like you blessed me. You see, I was in the Hospital and very sick, and you came with pastor Agustin and prayed for me. The Lord healed me at that time, and this is my way to thank Jesus for your service toward me. I am blessed to bless you."

We can always rely on His Word, for it gives us sufficient faith to receive His provision. Many times, before we call He has already answered, for He said, *Before they call I will answer; while they are still speaking I will hear.*

◆   ◆   ◆

This last story is so important that the Lord gave a vision of it beforehand. In a sense, the vision was an unfolding of my life. In it, I was attacked with the intention of taking my life, yet I decided not to defend myself, but to allow the enemy to kill me. Just as I was about to take my last breath, I told the attackers that I forgave them and that Jesus forgave them. With those words, not only was I healed instantly, but I arose with a new power from the Holy Spirit. When someone asked me what happened, I told them that it was the *Power of No Retaliation*. This made me think of Jesus, who, having all power, decided not to use it in order to bring salvation to mankind.

With that as introduction, I now tell you of the suffering of my own Kidron Valley. Its agony is difficult for me to describe; and no dainty philosophy can heal its wounds. Yet from ancient times we are told to ... *not despise the chastening of the Lord, nor be discouraged when you are rebuked by Him; for whom the Lord loves He chastens, and scourges every son whom He receives ...* If *It was fitting for Him, for whom are all things and by whom are all things, in bringing many sons to glory, to make the captain of their salvation perfect through sufferings ...* who *though He was a Son, yet He learned obedience by the things which He suffered ...* then we, too, must be willing to say with Job *Though He slay me, yet will I trust Him.* Even so, the chastening of the Lord is dreadful. If you think not, look again at the suffering of the Lamb.

The Kidron Valley is the modern Wadi en-Nar, also know as the fire Wadi, a torrent bed located at the north of Jerusalem that reaches the way of the wilderness and ends up in the Dead Sea. It is a dry, sun baked riverbed that is filled with water only for short periods in the rainy season. It is also called the Valley of Jehoshaphat. It could have other names like the Baptism of Suffering, like the one the Lord took before going to Calvary. It was not only for Jesus, but also for those who follow His steps, for it is a place for cleansing the temple, and, since we are the temple of the Holy Spirit, sooner or later every true disciple of Jesus enters the Kidron Valley.

Several years ago, it was my turn. I could not have imagined the pain. Yet, one thing stood out: I had a choice, for though the Holy Spirit led me to the valley, it was my choice to step in or pull back. I chose to enter just like Jesus did when He surrendered to the will of the Father and drank the cup of suffering. The reason for the valley is to cleanse the soul, to make it a partaker of Jesus' holiness, and thus, a tool of His grace. In the Bible, when a godly king began to reign, he cleansed the temple by burning the utensils of desecration in the Kidron Valley. After that, true worship was re-established.

Today many Christians are unaware of this, and therefore never become servants that will fulfill God's will in their lives. They are powerless in the service of the Lord. This valley for you will be an area that you are comfortable with and secure in; but it suddenly will collapse before your eyes. You cannot do anything about it. It could be your marriage, business, family or ministry, but you will be tested to the fullest.

In my case was it the breaking of a 25 year marriage and of a loved one going home. It started on a mission trip to the Philippines. My wife, saying she had no leading from the Lord, did not go. So I took Victor, a good and faithful brother. We went to Mindanao. And, as I started to preach I found that the anointing of the Holy Spirit was not there. So I closed the meeting with prayer and went to fast and pray for the next day. Normally I do all my fasting before I go into a trip, so this was unusual. The next day as I started to minister, the Holy Spirit led me to a song about the potter and the clay. As I finished the Lord impressed me to sing it again. So I did. And again. I felt the Lord telling me to repeat the song. Then I realized that I was singing it to myself; the calling of the song was to die to self. I told the Lord that I thought I had taken care of that long before, when I asked Him to come into my life. He seem to say, "Never mind you must do it." I started to weep and I told the Lord whatever it meant, I would do it. As soon as I spoke those words, the anointing of the Holy Spirit fell in such a way that, with no further word, the people started to repent and ask Jesus into their lives. A true revival broke out.

Later, we went to an island the Gospel had not reached, except for one part of a family a precious pastor, Julieta Chua, had witnessed to. I remember how the Holy Spirit fell there. New souls were saved and many healings took place. I remember as we gave the invitation it took several minutes for someone to respond, but the Holy Spirit had laid on my heart that many souls would be saved that night. Finally an elderly lady stepped forward and was miraculously healed. She was the first of many. It was a fruitful trip: souls were saved, healed and delivered; and a true manifestation of the Holy Spirit occurred.

I was happy on my return home, but little did I know what was waiting ahead: My Kidron Valley.

It happened like this. On a trip, while in Miami, I called my wife into our room to relate my feelings to her. I told her how much I loved her and what she meant to me, but that there was something she seemed to have forgotten: that my love for Jesus was greater; that nothing could stand in the way of that love. But she had changed toward me and the ministry. It was like being married to a different person. Who was to blame, I could not tell. I know there was a lack of communication on my part, especially when she tried to share her feelings. It takes two to have an open dialogue to save a marriage. She had come to the end of her rope and I had not even seen it.

Within three days of our return home, as I was driving, the Holy Spirit came over me. I stopped the car and told the Lord I was ready to drink of that cup. The following day my wife left, never to return. Immediately I went into an emergency fast, no food or drink, not even water until I heard from the Lord.

It did not take long. Within two days and a half, as I poured my heart out to the Lord, the peace of God flooded my being, and before my eyes appeared the face of Alejandra, a precious sister in the Lord that I had met in previous trips to Mexico. This startled me, but I remained in that peace. Then I hear the voice of the Lord saying to me: "Carlos you can marry again or take your wife back." Those words went through me like a sword, dividing soul and spirit. I pondered deeply. For a few seconds, I could not think of what to answer. My words were: "Lord, you know that since I met you I have not even looked to another woman. I love this woman, I would like to have her back. But I am not going to choose. You choose for me. The only thing I ask is that when I am not under this peace, do not pay attention to me." I knew that my flesh would fight, but I wanted Jesus to take over completely. On the one hand, my wife, whom I loved, had chosen to walk outside the counsel of the Word of God; and on the other, I hardly knew Alejandra. The only connection I could think of was that once when I was ministering in Mexico City I saw her worshipping the Lord, and that caught my attention. I told the Lord that if something happened in my life and I had to marry again I would pick someone like her.

The two best decisions I ever made were, first, when I asked Jesus to come into my heart, and second, when I let Him make this choice. He chose Alejandra for me. Later, when I told Alejandra about the vision, she said I had made a great impression on her since she met me, and that she had told the Lord that the person she would choose to marry had to have a call for service like mine. She also said that she had planned, in the day of her marriage, to ask me to perform the ceremony.

We decided we would not push the issue that we would wait on the Lord. I was not going to seek a divorce or even participate in any part of it; and further, if there were repentance on the part of my wife, I would reconsider the matter. The Lord gave a timetable. He said that the issue would be resolved in six months. I continued fasting, and it happened exactly as He said. She divorced me at six months. I was not present when the divorce finalized. Alejandra and I married six months later.

I believe that growing while you are going through the valley is what counts; not merely going through. The lesson I learned was priceless. I learned more of the character of Jesus in those six months than in eighteen previous years. This valley could also be call the valley of humiliation. I remember that the Holy Spirit commanded me not to open my mouth to defend myself, or to let any root of bitterness take hold of my life. Always forgiveness and mercy had to be practiced on a daily basis.

In this Kidron valley experience, not only had my ex-wife departed, but several close associates in my ministry also left. It was during that time that I reached out for help from some precious saints. These blessed homes became cities of refuge for me. First I went to see Dan and Mary Pratt, who deeply love our Lord Jesus Christ. During the conversation, Mary discerned my pain and said: "Carlos, you have come from the battle field in a foreign country, and you are a wounded soldier. Let us fast and seek the Lord for you; you need to rest." Those words were comfort from on high.

Also, during that time, Olga and Harry Llenza invited me to stay with them any time I needed. I remember the many hours they spent with me in prayers, seeking the Holy Spirit for answers. And others also reached out to me during the pain of those months. Once, when Agustin Enriquez and I were on the way to Miami we stopped in Stuart, at the home of Rick and Beverly Crary. As soon as they saw me, they were full of compassion. Beverly said, "Stay here and let us dress your spiritual wounds." I remember waking up in the middle of the night in the home of Mike and Fredy Alayon, knocking on their bedroom door, and Fredy getting up to pray for me. In Mexico City, I used to sleep downstairs in the home of Jose and Eva Galvez. Jose came down and took me upstairs to a room next to them to keep me close for prayer during the night hours.

During this travail, the Holy Spirit caused me to remember a pastor in Veracruz named Neftali. When I was ministering there, he came to me heavily burdened. His wife had left him and had taken their daughter with her. He went to get his daughter back, and when he came to see me he was running for his life. The Lord asked me if I remembered that time. I said, "Yes." Then He said, "You prayed for him," but then He asked me, "How would you pray now?" I paused for a minute and then said, "Lord I would not pray. I would only hold him next to me and cry with him."

And, if the divorce wasn't enough, my darling Mother (who was a comfort and pillar of strength all my life) also died. This was woe upon woe. Just when I needed her most, she was gone. I felt so very alone. I remember that I went to the Chapel in the funeral home about 30 minutes before the memorial service I was going to conduct on her behalf. I decided to move around the Chapel and lay hands on each chair. My prayer was simple but from the heart, "Dear Jesus, don't let my feelings get involved with the preaching." I knew there would be a lot of people, for my mother was dearly loved in the Spanish community. As I approached the last pew, I couldn't hold back the tears. I was hurting inside. I desperately missed my mother, for, after I led her to salvation she became a powerful intercessor for me. Yet, now I faced this difficult time so very alone. The divorce was humiliating and painful. As I felt these emotions, I could refrain no longer. I cried out unto the Lord, "Is there no one to hold my hands, to pray for me?"

I needed someone right then.

At that moment the door of the Chapel opened. A lady approached me with her daughter. She said, "Carlos, you don't remember me, but five years ago I was in the hospital dying. You came to pray for me. The Lord healed me and, though I did not receive salvation at that time, your words never departed from my heart until the day I accepted Jesus as my Savior, and not only I, myself, but my daughter as well." At first, I was speechless. Then I realized what Jesus was accomplishing. Not only was He sending her to hold my hand in prayer, but also He was showing me that I had planted the seed of the Word. Words came to me *Cast your bread upon the waters for after many days you will find it again.* From that moment, the Holy Spirit comforted me in such a way that when the time came to preach I had the mind of Christ, and many received Jesus into their hearts.

Juan Hirmas came to Mother's funeral to be with me. Juan, whom I had led to Jesus several years before, was walking with me to the graveside when the Lord spoke to me and said, "Carlos, when you bury you mother, you will bury your marriage as well." I replied, "Jesus, you know what is best. Do as you wish." The next day, I called my stepdaughter from Houston and asked her, "Did you go with your mother at 2:45 PM yesterday before the judge to finalize the divorce? She said, "Yes, but how did you know?" I told her the Lord told me the precise time it took place.

About ten days later, I had a visit from an angel of God in a dream. I asked why my mother's death had to be at the same time as the divorce? His answer was, "Was she not an intercessor in your life and ministry?" I said. "Yes." Then he proceeded to tell me the first words she spoke as she faced Jesus, "Lord take the burden from my son's life, please. I don't think he can take much more." That was the coronation of her intercession for her son, face to face with Jesus as a mother.

Another angel, who had a golden censer, came and stood at the altar. He was given much incense to offer, with the prayers of all the saints, on the golden altar before the throne.

These demonstrations of love were hidden manna that kept me going. They protected the ministry the Lord had given, and made it possible for me to be where I am today. Many have been saved and touched because of that love and concern. These homes were like cities of refuge to me.

To wrap up this matter: I was in Tlanepantla, Mexico, at the home of Jose Galvez. As I was waking up, I had a dream of my ex-wife. She was holding a log burning at both ends. I was trying to keep her from being burned. I asked the Holy Spirit for the interpretation. He said: "Carlos you are an unfaithful servant." At those words I covered my face in shame, for I knew He was right. I had been ministering the Word in Tlanepantla for two weeks, but had been holding back in the area of deliverance, even though there was a strong need for it. This was wrong, for deliverance is part of my ministry, as it should be every believer. There was no excuse; I was holding out on purpose. Secretly it had to do with my feelings toward the Lord. I was hurt and still had animosity toward my wife, and especially the man who had invaded my marriage. Even though I'd forgiven them, I was still deeply wounded.

Immediately after the Lord's rebuke, I dropped to the floor and asked Him to forgive me. Then I asked Him to heal me; then I wept. After I went back to bed I had a vision of the man who had taken my rightful place. He was before me; I could almost touch him, as if it was not even a vision. Then Jesus asked: "Carlos, what do you want me to do with him?" Immediately I realized that He was giving me the power of life and death over that individual. I literally froze at the idea that so much power had been given to me. For a few seconds I was silent, then I said: "Lord, save his soul." Peace, love and mercy came over me. Then the most amazing thing happened: I was healed of a wounded heart, and delivered (for the rest of my life) from the thought of ever "getting even."

During that time the Lord gave me this verse: The war between the house of Saul and the house of David lasted a long time. David grew stronger and stronger; while the house of Saul grew weaker and weaker. In other words, the flesh was given way to the spirit, and habits were being broken. It was not easy, but during that time I learned in the school of the Holy Spirit, not only to be an overcomer, but also to remain as one.

Now I look back and realize that Jesus is not only an answer; He is *the* answer to all I need. The decision I made to let the Lord take over was the best decision I ever made. Alejandra has excelled in every area known to me. These days, when I introduce her I always say, "Alejandra is my crown ahead of time." I can truly say that all things work for the good to those that love Jesus.

Conclusion

I always read Jamie Buckingham's "Last Word," in the *Logos* magazine. It was consistently good. It reminded me that the last word belongs to God. Whenever I teach, preach or counsel, I always try to exit leaving the "Last Word" to God, usually by reading or quoting the Scriptures.

This book I have written is for those who have a longing (or need) to meet Jesus, the One and only One who can solve all their problems, no matter how large or small. The only condition is that they must have a willing and honest heart when seeking Him.

Jesus once told Simon the story of two debtors. One owed a lot, the other, a little. He asked Simon which of the two he thought would be most grateful for having his debt forgiven. Simon correctly answered that it would be the one with the larger debt. I know why I am so grateful to Jesus: I was forgiven much. The night I knelt at the foot of the cross and asked to be forgiven for my sin-laden past, He looked into my heart and accepted my confession.

Some have sought to accuse me for my past life. But, in truth, it is not even open for discussion, for that life has been covered by the blood of the Lamb. In addition, I have asked the people I hurt to forgive my transgression against them. And further, I have tried my best to show by the fruit of my new life that genuine repentance flows from deep within my heart. The bottom line for me is that I now serve Jesus, not out of obligation, but out of love. We cannot earn salvation; it is paid for in full by Jesus' blood. When you come to Him all that is needed is a true and repentant heart; the rest is for Jesus to finish.

978-0-595-47638-1
0-595-47638-4

Printed in the United States
100863LV00005B/376-558/A

9 780595 476381